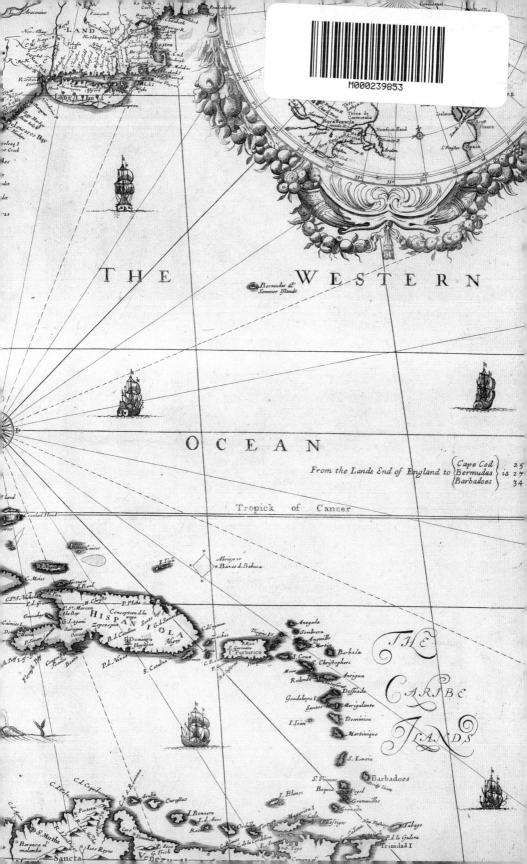

THE WESTERN

OCEAN

From the Lands End of England to (Cape Cod) 25
Bermudas) is 27
(Barbadoes) 34

Tropick of Cancer

THE CARIBE ILANDS

RUM
Curious

THE INDISPENSABLE
TASTING GUIDE
TO THE
WORLD'S
SPIRIT

RUM
Curious

THE INDISPENSABLE TASTING GUIDE TO THE WORLD'S SPIRIT

FRED MINNICK

VOYAGEUR
PRESS

Quarto is the authority on a wide range of topics.

Quarto educates, entertains and enriches the lives of our readers—enthusiasts and lovers of hands-on living. www.quartoknows.com

First published in 2017 by Voyageur Press, an imprint of The Quarto Group, 401 Second Avenue North, Suite 310, Minneapolis, MN 55401 USA. Telephone: (612) 344-8100 Fax: (612) 344-8692

QuartoKnows.com
Visit our blogs at QuartoKnows.com

Voyageur Press titles are also available at discount for retail, wholesale, promotional, and bulk purchase. For details, contact the Special Sales Manager by email at specialsales@quarto.com or by mail at The Quarto Group, Attn: Special Sales Manager, 401 Second Avenue North, Suite 310, Minneapolis, MN 55401 USA.

10 9 8 7 6 5 4 3 2 1

ISBN: 978-0-7603-5173-4

Library of Congress Control Number: 2017933002

ACQUIRING EDITOR: Jeff Serena
PROJECT MANAGER: Madeleine Vasaly
ART DIRECTOR: Laura Drew
COVER AND INTERIOR DESIGNER: BTDNYC

ON THE ENDPAPERS: *A New Map of the English Plantations in America, 1673, by Robert Morden.* BRIDGEMAN IMAGES
ON PAGES 2–3: *Sir Henry Morgan, namesake of Captain Morgan rum, defeats Spanish warships blocking the mouth of Lake Maracaibo in 1669.* BRIDGEMAN IMAGES
ON THE FRONTISPIECE: *Vintage promotional poster for Mauritius.* BRIDGEMAN IMAGES
ON THE DEDICATION: *A vintage advertisement by iconic Art Nouveau artist Alphonse Mucha.* ALAMY STOCK PHOTO

Printed in China

CONTENTS

Les Spécialités
J. & S. VIOLET Frères
BYRRH

TO
ANTI D'ORIGINE
ge et blanc
LLE RÉSERVE

Quelle Finesse !.. Quel Arôme !..
Ayez toujours sous la main
LE VRAI RHUM "BLOND"
DE LA MARTINIQUE.

VIN DOUX NATUREL
Spécialement sélectionné
pour la Femme de bon goût
SA CLASSE SURCLASSE

APÉRITIF A BASE DE V
AU QUINQUINA

Martin Cate

IT'S HARD TO UNDERESTIMATE THE IMPORTANCE OF RUM. Indeed, there has scarcely been a moment in the last three centuries when rum hasn't been at the center of commerce, nation building, wars at sea, or wars in court. No other spirit can tell so many tales of triumph and tragedy on its long journey alongside the development of the New World. It has transformed itself to match regional tastes, consumer demand, and commercial pressures. Often it has soared; at times it has fallen. It has enslaved and liberated. It has been a hero, a villain, and a scapegoat. But the story of rum goes on.

It's perhaps a cliché to declare that rum is at a crossroads. But today, in rum's fourth century, the dominance of a handful of players is being challenged. Beneath the headline-grabbing stories of rum wars between enormous producers over the fate of Cuban rum, you'll find a small but vocal handful of traditional Caribbean distillers raising their voices against what they see as the spread of homogenized industrial production globally. You'll find a diverse collection of American microdistilleries, now numbering in the hundreds, all keen to add their unique vision to the world of rum. And you'll find independent and merchant bottlers dedicated to sourcing some of the most interesting and unique casks in the world to showcase the products of traditional stills that seem ever endangered.

In this volume, Fred Minnick's concise history lays bare the complex evolution of this remarkable spirit and provides a clear guide to how we arrived at the intricate world of rum today. Minnick nicely illustrates the struggles and passions in the world of rum. But importantly, he is also unafraid to address the controversies in the industry directly. From regulatory questions to the cover-over tax, false or misleading age statements, sugar and other additives, and much more, no contentious issue goes unaddressed. Consumers will benefit from a

OPPOSITE: *1960s advertising for J. and S. Violet.* BRIDGEMAN IMAGES
FOLLOWING SPREAD: *Îles des Saintes, Guadeloupe.* SHUTTERSTOCK

greater understanding of these issues; beyond the debates, they will also benefit from some clear explanations of the methods of production and how they affect taste, character, and body. Often, there is so little to glean from vague and minimal labeling that you can find yourself at best guessing the contents of a bottle. And Minnick and I share a passion for abandoning the hoary shibboleth of white, gold, and dark as a rum classification method. Hopeless and outmoded, it does nothing to explain the distillation methods used.

For those of us who, as retailers, are faced daily with decisions about what rums to present to our guests and what rums work best in our cocktail programs, information and transparency are sometimes rare but always vital components of our efforts. At Smuggler's Cove, the hundreds of members of our rum club, the Rumbustion Society, are passionate about understanding both the art and the science that underpin the spirit in each bottle, and it's my responsibility to help

them become the most educated consumers they can be. We're proud to have worked closely with many of the brands discussed herein to make that a reality.

There is clearly a struggle for the soul of rum. And books like the one in your hands are vital for consumers to better understand the magnificently diverse but often baffling nature of this wonderful spirit. Yet, despite the confusion, rum has a way of creating the most ardent devotees. Even a cursory glance at many of the online forums dedicated to it will reveal powerful emotions and fervor for the spirit. It's the passion that surrounds rum that makes it so engaging and exciting for many around the world. Let this book help ignite a fire in you. Each sip contains multitudes. Drink it in deeply.

MARTIN CATE is the author of *Smuggler's Cove* and owner of the San Francisco bar of the same name.

RUM: THE SPIRIT OF THE FUTURE

RUM EVOKES A CERTAIN VACATION MINDSET. Your toes in the sand with a stiff, fruity rum drink in your hand, the ocean breeze cooling your skin, or wearing a Hawaiian shirt while looking over a cruise ship's bow . . . that's the rum life. No spirit embodies a sense of place like rum. Much of the good stuff is distilled, aged, and bottled within a quick drive from the ocean, so this sense of place is genuine and organic to this beautiful spirit.

But rum means so much more than a fruity vacation cocktail. It influenced empires and presents complicated flavor profiles when sipped neat. It was a bargaining chip in the creation of the United States and had a reputation so delightful that George Washington purchased barrels for his personal consumption. Unfortunately, the marketing of rum focuses on gimmicks, leading to mass confusion over how rum is defined and what it contains. In the basic US federal definition, rum comes from sugarcane. Yet, there's a Kentucky sorghum-molasses rum and a Colorado sugar-beet "rum." How can they be called rum if not from a sugarcane base? Somehow, the US federal government has allowed these labels—a damn crime to many of us rum lovers.

The sad fact is that traditional, true rum is going extinct, and the US government is largely to blame. The United States subsidizes the Virgin Islands' distilleries and allows a cover-over tax, which allows these islands and Puerto Rico to keep the federal excise taxes. Many opponents believe this has led to corrupt island governments and caused tax experts to suggest that some distillers incur no cost to produce subsidized rum. This all goes back to the 1917 US acquisition of Saint Thomas, Saint Croix, and Saint John Island. Today, it's one big money

PRECEDING SPREAD: *A seventeenth-century engraving depicting a sugar refinery in the French Antilles.* BRIDGEMAN IMAGES

OPPOSITE: *Rum's origins are connected to the Caribbean islands, which often conjure ideas of daiquiris near the shore. Not far from these sandy Saint Lucian beaches, rum distilleries produce some of the world's best rum.*

grab. In 2015, President Barack Obama released $211 million in cover-over payments to the Virgin Islands for the 2016 fiscal year. (More on cover-over and subsidies in the history section.)

The presence of this subsidized rum has also led to retail shelf spaces being dominated by certain styles of rum. In too many cases, the flavored rums and those made at industrial-scale facilities "own" shelf space in liquor stores, because these rums are supported with significant marketing dollars pipelined down to the distributor, who sets up point-of-purchase materials in liquor stores and bars. And since the fruity vacation reputation pervades the public's perception of rum, great sipping rum struggles to compete with brandy and whiskey for the aficionado's palate. More importantly, novice consumers think that rum's flavor profile is that of Captain Morgan, that premium "white" is Bacardi, and that a sipping rum is Cruzan Single Barrel—because these are the products they see, buy, and taste. A random liquor store or bar in Boise, Idaho, will not have Hampden, Rhum Barbancourt, or even a more widely distributed Mount Gay—all rums still distilled with methods used in the old days.

But as is often the case in today's world, passionate rum consumers are causing something of a civil war in the social media trenches and at industry events, fighting over rum's traditional styles and the spirit's meaning.

While there are many great rum distilleries, the public perception is that the larger brands adulterate their rums postdistillation, and that they deceive consumers with fake age statements and misleading fanciful terminology, such as *single barrel* and *solera*. But nothing gets in the rum nerd's craw more than adding sugar.

The rub, of course, is that it's all legal under US guidelines. Many say that the flavor-adding practice is steeped in tradition for South American rum makers. Others, though, say that adding wine, port, or sugar is a way to hide bitterness from the barrel, and that these sweetened rums are therefore inferior to nonmodified rum. More than anything, consumers want transparency, proper labeling, and the same respect which is afforded to whiskey and brandy distillers. In comparison to other spirits, where the distillers remain silent, rum's antisugar league is very vocal.

Foursquare master distiller Richard Seale adheres to what he calls the old way of making rum, which is to pot and column distill the fermented molasses or pressed cane and age it in the barrel, and then to blend the pot-and-column-aged rums when it's time to bottle. In Seale's ideal world, rum distillers don't include additives postdistillation. He calls the larger, bigger-brand rums coming from column stills "industrial rum" and says one cannot taste the difference between their rums and vodka. "That's a problem when you can't taste the difference between rum and vodka," he says. Seale has adopted the classification recommendation from Luca Gargano of Velier, in Italy, in which unadulterated rum is separated from the sugared-up rum. The reason for a taste similarity between some rums and vodka is that many rum distillers are using the same techniques as they do with vodka, which the US government defines as an "odorless" and "tasteless" spirit. Rum is meant to have rich flavor, both from its fermentation base and the barrel, so staunch distillers and rum lovers consider the vodka-style rums to be an insult to the historic category.

> ## Gargano's Proposed Rum Categories
>
> - **PURE SINGLE RUM**—pure pot-distilled rum, a direct analog to "single malt" or Cognac.
> - **SINGLE BLENDED RUM**—a blend of rums from the pot still and the traditional column still, analogous to blended Scotch whiskey.
> - **TRADITIONAL RUM**—rums from traditional column distillation, similar to grain whiskey.
> - **RUM**—rums from modern multicolumn alcohol plants.

Even more insulting is the lack of disclosure from some brands, which damage the category's stature in the eyes of truth seekers, who are not afraid to publicly call out writers, distillers, or brand ambassadors. The scenario goes something like this:

RUM NERD: Do you have sugar in your rum?

BRAND AMBASSADOR: No, of course not. This is pure distillate, using only the finest sugarcane known to man and only the purest water. It's aged in American oak with a deep rum char and artfully rests under the Caribbean sun. Zeus came from the heavens to sneeze on this rum as it went into the bottle.

Rum nerd pulls out a hydrometer, which looks like a plastic stapler, sticks it in the rum, and shows the sugar percentage.

RUM NERD: You're a liar.

BRAND AMBASSADOR: Um, I uh . . . I'm unaware of this. Let me call the distiller.

In various forums, whether online or in person, the above scenario has played out many times. It doesn't help that the Swedish and Finnish governments also test for sugar traces in rum and post the results online, which are then republished by blogs and this book. So, it's probably not a good idea to hide your sugar; in the Internet age, people will find out. Despite this growing desire for transparency, many rum brands continue to deny the use of sugar, while others fully embrace all production styles of rum.

Those who do disclose their sweetness find that many welcome them with open arms. You'll not find a more popular brand (among the rum nerds) in the United States than Plantation, which argues that the addition of sugar to rum is no different than dosage in champagne. Plantation owner and master blender Alexandre Gabriel stands by the sugar tradition that's been so widely used in Guatemala and Venezuela. He believes the technique even adds a touch of complexity to the rum. "There are so many ways to achieve great rum, just as there are so many different styles of cooking," says Gabriel, who then uses the analogy of a Frenchman finding Jamaican food unpalatable. "Does that make the Jamaican food no good? No, it just means the Frenchman doesn't care for Jamaican food."

But those who make rum similar to Seale's Foursquare agree that there needs to be classification separation. Although not as vocal as Seale, legendary Appleton Estate master blender Joy Spence believes what she calls "true rum" should be categorically separated from those with flavoring, which Spence refers to as "flavored rum. . . . If you want to add sugar to rum, then you move it into the flavored rum category. True rums are rums that derive flavor from sugarcane and the process of fermentation, distillation, and aging. You want to add sugar? You can, but the two should be separated."

Of course, it's important to point out that some brands use minimal amounts of sugar, while brands such as Zacapa are tested to be in the range of twenty grams per liter. They're also not simply adding sugar cubes—they're adding honey, wine, and other spirits. Some might actually have the sugar equivalent to qualify as liqueurs, and others will still find acceptance in the rum-centric community.

With that said, postdistillation additives are hardly rum's biggest problem. In 2015, *Munchies* reporter Clarissa Wei exposed Nicaraguan rum's connection to the deaths of sugarcane workers. Wei's story, "The Silent Epidemic Behind Nicaragua's Rum," cited research that indicated between 2,800 and 3,500 people have died from chronic kidney disease over the past decade. "It's a disease that researchers have linked to working conditions at the sugarcane mill," Wei wrote.

In the story, Flor de Caña was the only brand connected, thereby sparking a revolt against the popular brand. Renowned mixologists and bar owners engaged in a national boycott and significantly damaged the brand's reputation. The most public display came from a Houston bar, Anvil Bar and Refuge, which dumped twenty bottles down the drain, with owner Bobby Heugel making the following Facebook posting: "Should the bar industry formally boycott Flor de

Rum is made all over the world, but the celebrated tradition was set in the Caribbean islands, where tropical mountains, azure waters, and never-ending vegetation arouse all the senses. APPLETON ESTATE JAMAICA RUM

Caña? I don't know. But, if you feel comfortable pouring a rum that is so explicitly documented to have deadly effects on the people who produce it, I don't know where your moral compass is at."

Flor de Caña responded with a broader picture of the situation, essentially addressing it as an international problem, with chronic kidney disease breakouts in Mexico, Guatemala, El Salvador, Honduras, and Costa Rica. Flor de Caña supports ongoing studies to fix chronic kidney disease, the company says.

From a historical perspective, this is par for the course. Rum's connections to savage pirates and slavery make it the world's most infamous spirit. But for the most part, other than an occasional boycott, consumers do not care about the unsavory past. They're mostly hung up on labeling.

Rum can be made anywhere in the world, and its production methods vary by country. However, no entity is currently holding companies liable for improper rum labeling, as occurred with Colorado's sugar-beet rum. Despite the US

Made in Danville, Kentucky, Wilderness Trail's Harvest Rum comes from sorghum molasses (as stated on the label). US federal regulations define rum as being from sugarcane, not sorghum. But Wilderness Trail's Pat Heist says, "Harvest Rum is made from molasses condensed from the juice of a cane grass in the same family as sugar cane. Sorghum cane, however, is not the same as sugar cane, which is required for rum production, depending on how you interpret the regulations. Our product is a spirit distilled from fermented sorghum cane molasses that is labeled as a rum. It's definitely a debatable topic."

rum definition requiring a sugarcane base, Stoneyard Colorado Rum, made with sugar beets, was allowed to be labeled as rum.

Despite such examples, there's no excuse for the lack of disclosure and blatant attempts to deceive consumers.

Many brands place numbers on labels, making it appear to be an age, when in reality the number represents absolutely nothing. Rum types are also a bit deceiving. Light rum is also called white or silver, but the label merely means it has no color. Many light rums were indeed aged upward of five years but are colorless simply because the distillers filtered out the color. Meanwhile, gold rum, amber rum, and dark rum are aged rums that have coloring added to make them appear darker. So, the entire consumer-based system of rum identification is based on food coloring. "Does anybody really know how much coloring is being added to their rum?" asks Bailey Pryor, who founded the Real McCoy rum line, which bottles Foursquare rum. "We should be speaking aged versus unaged, and dry (no sugar added) versus sweet style."

This debate, while ongoing, has no possible conclusion, no compromise, no international regulation strengthening the transparency, and no rum organization that prevents fraudulent representation. Rum is bottled in more than fifty countries, which is what gives us so many styles and unique flavor profiles. It is also what offers a beautiful spirit from which to debate the finer points of distillation, aging, using fermented sugarcane juice versus molasses, and the ongoing and often-heated discussion of sugaring.

That's what *Rum Curious* offers you—a sneak peek into the styles of rum. My intent is to deliver a guide with a touch of history, production information, cogent tasting notes, scores, and classic and contemporary cocktails to help you make wise rum-purchasing decisions. It's my opinion that the best rums do not contain sugar, but as you will see in my tasting notes, there are some rums with additives that are of high quality. In the Appendix, where possible, I provide sugar content, off-the-still proof, barrel-entry proof, and as much production detail as I possibly can. Many distillers and tasters will say these are not "end all, be all" measures for understanding how and why a rum tastes the way it tastes, and I agree with that view. There are also fermentation temperatures and duration, distillation temperature, sea proximity, yeast strains, and dozens of other factors that go into rum. But we have to start somewhere, and in this book I have provided as many details as was practical.

I have split up the tasting section into the categories of Unaged, Aged, Flavored, and Other Cane Spirits. In the age of information, rum consumers should not be forced to base purchasing decisions off the amount of food coloring in the bottle—white, gold, and dark. Although white, gold, and dark labels are never going away, I hope this book will educate consumers on what is what. I have also included cocktails that will be fun to make at home.

This book may challenge your perception of rum and introduce you to products new to you. You may learn why rum, if properly managed, is the brown spirit of the future.

Yes, rum belongs on the beach and in fruity drinks, but it is a delectable sipper and pairs beautifully with cigars.

PART ONE

About Rum

CHAPTER 1

A SHORT HISTORY

CAPTAIN MORGAN AND HIS CREW walk down a dark, damp cave, where bountiful treasure awaits. Their torches flicker, and they toast with rum.

In another adventure, a navy encounters Morgan and his scallywags, but Morgan walks to the plank and dives into the ocean. They toast with rum.

With his long hair, swashbuckling hat, and saber, Morgan is clearly a pirate. Women love him; British sailors despise him.

In 1661, Captain Morgan takes the hand of a fair princess as they dance beneath candlelit chandeliers and run toward a secret door, down a spiral staircase toward snakes and seduction. It's a party, away from the dignitaries, and . . . they toast with rum.

These are all commercials for the rum brand Captain Morgan, but there's truth in them, too. Rum is connected to pirates, scallywags, and the British navy, and you might even find a serpent or two.

The real pirates were often gruesome murderers who plundered ships for treasure, including rum, as early as the mid-1600s, when rum is thought to have first been distilled. They sailed the open waters between Madagascar and New York, near the Caribbean islands, and near major port cities, waiting for merchant ships to board and loot.

These were not church-going people by any means, but some remained quite incognito and attempted to avoid bloodshed.

In 1696, pirates boarded the merchant ship *Nassau* with Captain Giles Shelly aboard—only they didn't come with guns blazing. The *Nassau* was loaded with Jamaican rum, Madeira wine, and gunpowder, and the pirates appeared as

PRECEDING SPREAD: *Haughton Court, Hanover, Jamaica, circa 1820.* BRIDGEMAN IMAGES
OPPOSITE: *Pirates have a long-standing tradition in rum. They drank it, stole it, and murdered for it. Today, rum has several pirate-named brands, such as Sailor Jerry, Admiral Nelson, Captain Morgan, and Lady Bligh—enough positions for a whole fleet and a landlubber too!* BRIDGEMAN IMAGES

educated merchants who traded. Under cover, they stole the *Nassau*'s goods. Nobody would have known of this endeavor had the pirates not consumed a great deal of rum at port and bragged about their adventures.

The more aggressive pirates sailed under forged commissions from the French and Spanish. They boarded ships armed, stole the booty, and took the clothes of travelers. The merchant-ship captains and crews were stripped and marooned on nearby islands or murdered. In 1805, a British captain shared the story after pirates captured the ship *Shannon*:

> It is with much regret I have to inform you of the melancholy and unfortunate circumstance that happened to me on board the *Shannon*, on the 1st day of December last, in my passage up the Gulf, near the island of Polior, after a short but pretty smart engagement with fifteen pirate dows and botillas. At three in the afternoon they boarded the *Shannon* with swords and spears in hand, and I am sorry to acquaint you that I had one man killed outright, and four more severely wounded, besides myself. You will be sorry to learn that I have had my left hand taken off at the wrist, my left shoulder dislocated, and eight wounds in my body. In this deplorable state, being stripped quite naked, I lay eight days weltering in my gore, exposed to the weather, not being permitted to go below. I was fortunate in getting some biscuit and a few bottles of wine the next day, but the crew were not allowed any fire or food for three days.

Even with these stories of horror, some pirates were beloved, bringing in untaxed spices and duty-free teas to the Americas without the British knowing. And some were practically country founders; pirate-obtained contraband helped build Belize.

Pirates were men, women, and former slaves from all established countries. They were free on the open sea, always seeking ships to rob in some fashion. Fiction and fanciful tales would call this treasure hunting, and sometimes pirates were so-called privateers, but the British navy despised pirates and preferred calling them thieves. Navies around the world were under constant threat and at war with the likes of Blackbeard, Captain Morgan, William Kidd, and others— many of whom were American—who would be immortalized in stories, and always with rum. One example is the old sea song from Robert Louis Stevenson's classic novel *Treasure Island*: "Fifteen men on the dead man's chest—Yo-ho-ho, and a bottle of rum!"

Newspapers published poems celebrating pirating, often championing pi- rates as truly free men. "Hurrah! The land's the home of the Slaves / Freedom bides only on the Waves!" ran the words of W. Grey A——N in "The Pirate's Roundelay" in the *Sydney Morning Herald*, 1833.

When they weren't drinking it, pirates used rum to barter or converted it into cash. Pirates and rum are so intertwined that Turkish pirates were connected to rum in 1634, some thirty years before rum became widely known. According to the 1878 book *A Short History of Penzance*, as well as other nineteenth-century books, Saint Ives fishermen encountered busted pirate ships. Many of the Turkish pirate crew were lost or had been enslaved.

Slaves were used in the Caribbean Island sugar plantations, where rum was made. Sugarcane is a labor-intensive crop. Most Caribbean slaves came from Ireland and Africa.
LIBRARY OF CONGRESS

The fishermen found barrels of rum, according to this book's alleged verified account. The pirates paid locals with rum to fix their ships. "What the fishermen did with the rum history does not declare. I suppose they drank some, and sold the rest to the 'licensed victuallers [*sic*] of the period,'" the book indicates.

It's impossible to know if this story is accurate. Perhaps the pirates carried barrels of distilled spirit, such as brandy, and historians later assumed it was rum. After all, it was their drink of choice.

With that said, the spirituous debate of rum's origins requires a closer look at sugarcane.

RUM'S ORIGINS

Long before a pirate girded his saber and swung across the ship's bow, that tall, tan-and-green perennial grass, sugarcane, changed the world. Like many of the early crops, sugarcane's exact discovery date is hotly debated. Sugar scholars disagree on its botanical history, and the theories are separated by a few thousand years. India, China, and New Guinea have all been linked to sugarcane's discovery between five thousand and eight thousand years ago, since each region's ancient people harvested sugarcane for food. In ancient Chinese literature, a man named Gu Kaizhi started chewing on cane stalk until his teeth sunk deep into the sweeter roots, where he found "better realms."

Perhaps the most notable early discovery of sugarcane comes from the expeditions of Alexander the Great, whose unprecedented military campaign took troops through Asia and Africa. In 325 BC, Alexander the Great's admiral, Nearchus, referred to India's sugarcane as the "reeds that . . . produce honey, although there are no bees." These ancient sugarcane references are few and often confused with grain cultivations. It wasn't really until the Persians and Arabs created and perfected the refining of sugar in the seventh century that sugarcane's origins and benefits were studied more thoroughly.

In the eleventh and twelfth centuries, the Arabs introduced sugar to the Mediterranean region of Europe. Spain, Portugal, and Sicily embarked into sugarcane trade that transformed Europe while bolstering their power. The majority of the sugarcane was in Arab territories, where slaves were forced to cultivate cane for distribution throughout Europe. But the Portuguese explored the coast of Africa and discovered the Madeira Islands, Cape Verde, and the Canary Islands in the early fifteenth century. Sugarcane cultivation was possible here, and the Portuguese could produce sugar without Arab control. It was with sugar that the Portuguese could grow their power. The Portuguese enslaved Africans to conduct labor at the eighty sugar mills and two hundred plantations in Madeira, which became the world's biggest sugar exporter by 1500. This

Sugarcane was first discovered over five thousand years ago. It remains an important crop to the world (especially since it's used for rum). Today, sugarcane competes against corn and sugar beets for sweetener products. Rum, however, can only be made from sugarcane. These are sugarcane fields in Haiti. ADRIAN KEOGH

When Christopher Columbus landed in the New World, Spanish influence shaped the future of the West. SHUTTERSTOCK

production spread to the Canaries and Santiago in the Cape Verde islands, which required more rainfall for adequate sugarcane farming. By this time, the Spanish, Dutch, and English were seeking territories to cultivate their own sugarcane.

That's when Christopher Columbus introduced sugarcane to the West Indies, where the Spanish set up sugar mills in Cuba, Hispaniola, and Mexico. As the Portuguese did in Madeira, the Spaniards used African slaves as their primary labor force for sugarcane. The Portuguese continued their sugarcane expansion to Brazil, while the Dutch entered the slave trade to sell to those running sugarcane plantations. The Dutch also took control of Pernambuco, Brazil, in 1630 and embarked on their own sugarcane industry. By this time, the English colonies in the Caribbean were deeply rooted in sugar and slavery.

Slaves planted the sugarcane, fertilized it, cut stalks, and transported it to a mill, where the cane was crushed and juice extracted. They strained the juice and placed it in boiling pots until the sugar was crystalized. Slaves also seined the boiling matter to collect the molasses—the syrupy byproduct from making sugar. Their owners sold the sugar, but the molasses was set aside, where rainwater was added and it fermented naturally. Molasses could be sold and used as a sweetener too, but the fermented molasses was enjoyed by the slaves and by poor whites. At some point, somebody distilled this fermented molasses, and rum was born.

The earliest known spirit distillation using sugarcane comes in Brazil in the 1500s, where cachaça was distilled. Also called *pinga* or *aguardiente*, cachaça is distilled sugarcane juice. It was given to slaves and Indians, and cachaça became a currency for buying slaves too.

As for cachaça's distilled-molasses cousin, rum, the first records come in the seventeenth century. According to the 1651 account of Royalist refugee Richard Ligon, this libation was known as "kill-devil." Ligon lamented that "it lays" men asleep on the ground. Ligon's *A True and Exact History of the Island of Barbados* offers an interesting and early look at a sugar plantation and kill-devil's importance. He wrote, "if the stills be at fault, the kill-devil cannot be made." Ligon also wrote that "liquor" was mixed with chicken guts as a disease remedy. Despite its apparent occasional medicinal usage, kill-devil caused severe hangovers and made many people sick. (Maybe they didn't understand drinking responsibly in 1651?) Of course, the most likely reason for sickness is that they were drinking bad spirit. But Ligon also showed a slight bit of appreciation for the spirit, saying the earliest form of rum, combined with a cool breeze and tobacco, offered relief from the intense heat. Essentially, kill-devil was an alias for rum: it's more official titles were *rombustion*, appearing in a Dutch newspaper in 1652, and *rumbullion*, which was used to place an order in 1660 in Bermuda. While it's easy to see possible origins for the word here, one etymologist suggests that *rum* comes from an English and Dutch interpretation of the Romany word *rom*, defined as "excellent, fine and good."

ABOVE: *When this photo was taken in the 1940s, Caribbean rum was a burgeoning (and popular) spirit in the United States.* LIBRARY OF CONGRESS

OPPOSITE: *Most of the world's rum is produced in the Caribbean islands. Saint Lucia (pictured) was one of the early adopters of rum distilling and continues as the location of one of the most revered distilleries in the world.*

The spirit's many names, however, were not enough to shield them from legislation in the New World. The Puritan courts gave the order to confiscate "Barbados liquors, commonly called rum, kill devil or the like." All the Puritans could see was the intoxication aspect of rum. To this day, the teetotaler still does not appreciate the virtue in responsible consumption of spirit. Even with all of their rum heritage, the Caribbean islands do not fully embrace their spirit, with many religious institutions downplaying rum's importance and tourism agencies focusing on island beauty while often ignoring rum heritage.

Nonetheless, rum was the trending spirit in the 1700s. Distillers spoke of rum in the same breath as whiskey (distilled from grain) and brandy (distilled from fruit). Rum was a shilling a gallon cheaper than brandy and "cannot be distinguished by an extraordinary palate," wrote distiller George Smith in 1731. The distilling authorities of the time suggested using the inexpensive rum over brandy for rectification purposes, allowing for better profits. Rum's notoriety grew, and it was distilled wherever sugarcane grew. South America—especially Brazil—and the Caribbean islands were the primary rum-distilling regions, while the American colonies showed great promise in their enthusiasm for rum. In 1765, after Maryland rum defeated New England and Philadelphia rums in a competition, the salesmen Samuel and Robert Purveyance solicited potential buyers in the *Maryland Gazette*:

> Having furnished themselves with an expert distiller, and a plentiful stock of molasses, they propose to carry on the distilling business extensively, and to comply constantly the demand for home-made rum at nearly the same as the Philadelphia prices . . . The rum already made by them has been highly approved by the best judges, and deemed superior to either Philadelphia or New England Rum.

American colonists loved rum, consuming 3.7 gallons a year per person, and accepted the spirit as gifts from its politicians. When running for the Virginia House of Burgesses in 1758, George Washington supplied voters with 28 gallons of rum and 50 gallons of rum punch. Unfortunately, modern election laws prevent rum bribes at polling stations, but no wonder Washington was so beloved. Around 1765, America distilled some 4.8 million gallons of rum along the East Coast, making it more available than whiskey in major cities such as Boston. Rum also had a significant marketing advantage over its competitive spirits, brandy and whiskey—sailors. Starting in 1731, the British Royal Navy received a daily pint of Jamaican rum for each man and a half. The sailor rum ration decreased over time, but the tradition lasted until the 1970s. And apparently, that ration wasn't enough. Wherever the sailors ported, they sought rum. Jamaica, Saint Thomas, American ports, and others were fiscally encouraged to distill and sell rum to sailors. This immediate and constant demand from the world's most active navy encouraged businesses to create products for them. Merchant ships and the illicit ones fell in love with rum, too, using it for the sheer pleasure of drinking and as a valuable medicine.

In 1762, in *An Essay on the Most Effectual Means of Preserving the Health of Seamen, in the Royal Navy*, Dr. James Lind wrote that rum "proves the best and quickest restorative which a Sailor can have at Sea." Lind suggested sailors consume the rum in a punch. His recipe included fruits or fruit juice, vinegar-based shrubs, vegetable acid, cream of tartar, a half-pint of spirits, and a half-pint of water. "If the Officers, and others in the Ship, who make Use of Lemons or Oranges, would reserve the Peels to be put into the Spirits served to the Men, it would greatly improve the Flavor of the punch, and make it little inferior to what is made with Lemon Juice. I must add, that this is so innocent an Acid, that it may be taken in the Quantity of an Ounce or two," he wrote.

Rum was especially important to sailors stationed in North America, where men were exposed to new environments, allergens, and insects that caused frequent sickness. A 1757 letter sent to the British Parliament said that "it is death to drink beer or water in the field. Without a mixture of rum in the winter, it is

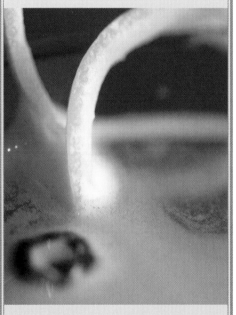

Grog

In the 1740s, Adm. Edward Vernon introduced water and rum to his sailors. They called this the *grog*, because Vernon wore a grogram cloak in rough weather. Grog became known as a mixture of any spirit with water, hot or cold, but later it became acceptable to mix with any juices. Rum remains the standard spirit for true grog.

Grog is a fun word to say, but it's even better to drink. Today's grogs often come with garnishes, a luxury the early sailors likely did not enjoy.

The British Sugar Islands comprised slaves and native workers who harvested sugarcane for the Crown and used its byproduct—molasses—for making rum. Many Caribbean rum companies still use horses and traditional tools to cut cane in some islands. LIBRARY OF CONGRESS

impossible to endure the cold." Rum was the medicine of the sea, used for curing swollen gums, distemper, sea scurvy, and diarrhea. Three spoonfuls would cure what ails ya; if it didn't, the doctors would give you a mixture of rhubarb and opium. Or you died.

Rum's medicinal prowess attracted apothecary wholesalers, who lined up at ports to purchase rum by the barrel. Mid-1700s-era pamphlets praised rum for being superior and of a "stronger union" than brandy, and it was described as more consistent and potent than whiskey. "For no spirituous liquor digests more kindly, or assists digestion more efficaciously than good rum, sufficiently diluted, and drunk in proper quantity," wrote Robert Dossie in *An Essay on Spirituous Liquors with Regard to Their Effects on Health*, in 1770. In fact, physicians and apothecaries of the time swore by rum's medicinal usage, driving an even greater economic reason for the world powers to plant sugarcane, refine sugar, and distill rum.

RUSH TO POWER

Rum and sugar were consequential to the British Empire, France, Spain, and the Americas. From the mid-1600s to the early 1800s, much of the world's economy revolved around sugar and its byproducts. Rum was just a small player in the world sugarcane grab but important nonetheless.

Of the major rum-production areas throughout the 1700s, the British controlled Jamaica, the Bahamas, Antigua and Barbuda, Saint Lucia, Barbados, and its Virgin Islands. The French owned Haiti, Grenada, and Saint Vincent. Spain used Cuba and Puerto Rico mainly for military purposes; rum was secondary. Denmark had Saint Croix, Saint John, and Saint Thomas. Although a secondary effort in comparison to military efforts, the islands were all vying for rum consumers at sea and in the American colonies, where rum distilleries could be found in Philadelphia, Baltimore, and New England. The eighteenth-century rum business study reveals an interesting trade war between France and England.

By the 1740s, the British sugar islands felt the competition, mostly from the French, whose sugar was exported into Europe without paying duties. The English, on the other hand, were forced to pay "very high" duties. The French were allowed to export sugars directly to foreign markets, while the English required their ships to enter home ports first. This allowed the French to carry goods to foreign markets quicker than the English and helped them gain a competitive advantage. The French also owned the island of Hispaniola, which enjoyed plentiful timber that made the English envious. The British sugar islands could not efficiently grow trees.

English businessman Thomas Salmon warned the Crown that Caribbean island disadvantages in comparison to the French were so many that "no English gentleman will be fond of having an estate in the Caribbean, or contribute much to promoting the sugar manufacturing there."

Around 1750, the American colonies were paying four shillings and eight pence for a gallon of French brandy and three shillings and eight pence per gallon of British island rum; this saving was not enough to discourage Americans from purchasing French spirits, which did not directly fatten the Crown's wallet. John Ashley wrote in *Memoirs and Considerations Concerning the Trade and Revenues of the British Colonies in America* that regulations should be imposed to fix rum at three shillings per gallon for duty and excises, and brandy at five gallons, "Thereby prevent the running of such great quantities of French Brandy or Rum."

These sugar and rum trade tensions arose around the same time that military action was first taken in the Ohio River Valley, which sparked the Seven Years' War (1754 to 1763). The war resulted in what's considered the first true world war, where the British and its allies were pitted against the French and its allies in a multicontinental conflict, including in North America, where it was dubbed the French and Indian War. This war greatly added to tensions between the British and American colonists.

King George III demanded American colonists help pay for the war debts. As part of the increased taxations upon the American colonies, many of whom were loyal British subjects, the Crown passed the Sugar Act of 1764, which forbade colonies from importing rum. The next year, Great Britain passed the Stamp Act, which required Americans to pay taxes on every piece of printed paper. Virginian Patrick Henry wrote that an American should possess the same liberties "enjoyed and possessed by the people of Great Britain."

The Americans protested the increased taxes with a simple slogan: "Taxation without representation." The Stamp Act was repealed in 1766, but the Sugar Act remained. Boats were frequently impounded for harboring smuggled molasses and rum. In 1771, the Portsmouth Molasses Party boarded the ship *Resolution* to save its one hundred hogsheads of smuggled molasses, an action that foreshadowed the Boston Tea Party two years later.

Tensions in the colonies continued to rise as Great Britain made sure through rule and action that the colonists knew they were subordinates to the Crown. When the British Parliament enacted the Tea Act of 1773, the British East India Company had a monopoly on tea trade in the colonies. With each tax increase or sanction, the colonists grew tired of British rule and revolted. Within three years, the colonies would sign the Declaration of Independence, with rum and molasses having major roles in creating America.

Today, the United States celebrates bourbon as "America's spirit," a designation from the 1964 Congressional Declaration that made bourbon whiskey a unique product of the United States. But due to its importance to colonial America, rum deserves equal consideration as "America's Spirit."

Nobody expresses rum's lost American sentiment better than Phil Prichard, who distills both rum and whiskey in Tennessee. "America's first rums were very different from the modern rums of the tropics. The first American rums were made from the same wonderful, sweet molasses that was used to make baked beans, brown bread, and Indian pudding. Molasses was the sweetener of choice of the early American settlers who poured it over their pancakes and cornbread; and since granulated sugar was either very expensive or nonexistent in the new American colonies, yes, it was even used by Martha Washington to make her apple pies," Prichard wrote.

Despite the First Lady using molasses—the same ingredient in America's first rums—in her apple pies, this country's legislators sealed rum's fate. And it wasn't good.

Lafayette Gingerbread

First Lady Martha Washington often used molasses in her cooking. And so did George Washington's mother. According to the Mount Vernon archives, Mary Ball Washington served a gingerbread cookie, made with molasses, to the Marquis de Lafayette when he visited her in Fredericksburg toward the end of her life. These cookies were named Lafayette Gingerbread. The recipe below is from George Washington's Mount Vernon, which is preserved and maintained by the Mount Vernon Ladies' Association.

Rum's most common base, molasses, is frequently used as a sweetener for baking. First Lady Martha Washington knew this and made some incredible desserts.

½ cup (1 stick) unsalted butter, softened

½ cup plus 2 tbsp. packed dark brown sugar

1 cup molasses

Scant 2¾ cups sifted all-purpose flour

1 tbsp. ground ginger

1 tsp. ground cinnamon

½ tsp. ground cloves

¼ tsp. ground allspice

2 large eggs, plus 2 large egg whites, lightly beaten

¼ cup fresh orange juice

1 tbsp. freshly grated orange zest

Fairy Butter for serving (optional—recipe available at www.mountvernon.org)

INSTRUCTIONS

1. Preheat the oven to 350°F. Butter a 9-inch-square cake pan.
2. In the bowl of an electric mixer, or in a large bowl beating by hand, combine the butter and brown sugar and beat until light and fluffy. Add the molasses, and continue to beat until well combined.
3. Sift the flour with the ginger, cinnamon, cloves, and allspice.
4. Alternately add the eggs and flour to the butter mixture, beating very well after each addition.
5. Add the orange juice and zest, and continue beating for several minutes until the batter is smooth and light.
6. Pour the batter into the prepared pan and bake for 35 to 45 minutes, or until a wooden skewer inserted in the center comes out clean. Set the cake on a rack to cool completely in the pan before slicing.
7. Serve squares of the cake spread with Fairy Butter, if desired.

WHISKEY WARS

Rum was an intended economic and cultural victim of the United States. As a country, the United States chose to encourage the development of whiskey over rum, perhaps to discourage duties being sent to Great Britain and to ameliorate farmer revenue sources for grains.

After George Washington enacted a whiskey tax, Pennsylvania distillers revolted in what was known as the Whiskey Rebellion. President Thomas Jefferson repealed the whiskey tax in 1802, but it briefly reappeared to pay for the War of 1812. From 1817 to 1862, American whiskey distillers did not pay taxes, while New England rum producers were highly taxed, and foreign spirits were impeded with high tariffs.

Upon the end of the War of 1812, the United States required a 20 percent duty on rum, sugar, and molasses from the British islands, as well as a $20 port charge. By 1822, Jamaican rum paid 75 percent tariffs, West Indies rum 110 percent, and molasses received tariff rates up to 30 to 40 percent. The Americans were systematically creating an economic disadvantage for rum distillers and importers. Consumers paid upward of 300 percent more for rum than whiskey, and New England distillers were forced to pay heavy duties on imported molasses. Meanwhile, whiskey and its base grains—specifically corn—were distilled tax free, and the government encouraged the planting of corn. New England rum makers and the rum importers reacted by petitioning Congress to drop its rum prejudice. Throughout the 1820s and 1830s, rum interests fought for their lives. "Whiskey has come into almost universal use throughout the United States, except those sections of the country which carry on a direct and barter trade with the West Indies," US Representative Samuel F. Vinton (Ohio–Whig) said in 1828. Vinton argued that rum was too expensive because of the labor and travel associated with it. But he argued that several states relied upon the West Indies for commerce. Vinton said,

> So the people of Maine and North Carolina can buy rum, because their lumber always finds a ready market in the West Indies. The fisherman can do the same thing, because he can always sell his fish in those Islands. But, sir, can the inhabitant of Maine or North Carolina send his lumber to Ohio or Kentucky? Will the people of Ohio, Kentucky, or Pennsylvania, give to the fisherman of Nantucket, their whiskey in exchange for his codfish? No sir, they will not do it, for the plain reason, that they do not want them. There is nothing that these people can send to the West to pay us for our whiskey. And until they can pay

us in their own labor or the produce of it, let the price of whiskey be what it may, ten, twenty, or thirty cents, the result will be the same; they cannot buy it. Communities of men and individuals must live by labor and the exchange of commodities, or they will go to inevitable ruin.

Vinton's American regional liquor argument provided hope that port cities could trade and barter with rum sellers while the whiskey states distilled whiskey. He did not believe in taxing molasses, saying "this tax upon molasses, like a killing frost, will be a curse to thousands, and a blessing to none."

Rum proponents began to argue that whiskey distillers were corrupt, buying grains below the farmer's costs and making a hefty profit. In the 1828 tariff bill, rum-friendly congressmen argued that taxes against foreign rum and molasses benefited whiskey distillers, while in defense of whiskey, other congressmen contended that every three gallons of imported molasses manufactured into New England rum eliminated the market for one American bushel of corn or rye.

Around the same time, Pennsylvania, Tennessee, and Kentucky whiskey were gaining notoriety, and their distillers were becoming wealthier by the year. Merchants had fewer requests for Jamaican rum and more for whiskey. In fact, during these congressional debates, the country's greatest liquor port city—New Orleans—saw fewer purchases of rum and more of whiskey. New Orleans newspapers consistently updated their readers when Kentucky whiskey shipments arrived, while barrels of rum waited for weeks before they were sold. So, it wasn't just legislative effort to kill rum in the United States. Americans wanted whiskey, and laws penalized rum producers so much that they could not compete on either price point or marketing.

As the United States became a whiskey nation, Congress passed multiple acts and declarations to preserve the country's whiskey heritage while trifling rum.

The British sugar islands continued to make rum, and the British Empire traded rum, molasses, tobacco, spices, and other goods from their colonies around the world. The rum producers, though, increasingly found themselves in a colonial relationship, in which they were secondary to the Crown. While the United States thrived in independence, the islands remained servants to the larger mother countries. Foursquare master distiller Richard Seale calls this the "colonial inferiority complex." Over time, some islands would become Third World countries and become known for their vacation resorts while their locals lived in poverty.

It's easy to see the hardship today, as many Caribbean locals live in shacks, while the lost distilleries are hidden. One not need to look further than the island

Larger distilleries are often considered factories. If properly managed, however, they can churn out some of the world's best rum.

nation that is perhaps the most heralded of them all—Jamaica. In 1893, Jamaica had 148 rum distillers. Today, there are five.

Furthermore, the several foreign-owned Caribbean distilleries that remain are towering, industrial facilities that are vastly different from the artisanal pot-still setups of the 1700s and 1800s.

The industrial demise of the Caribbean's rum regions didn't just happen overnight, and there are many other rum-making countries that endured these times. But rum's focal region has been and always will be the Caribbean, where rum's faltering corresponded to a drop in sugarcane demand.

In the mid-1800s, British businessmen heavily invested in the British sugar islands. J. Scott Bushe, the Colonial Secretary to Trinidad, wrote in 1883 that rum's trade increased the labor force. Bushe was encouraged by the sugar and rum growth in the islands but was deeply concerned with the US policy toward island sugar. The United States was now encouraging the sugar beet industry to decrease its reliance on foreign sugar. The country's change in sweetener was a "terrible blow to the present prosperity and future prospects of these islands."

As the United States and other countries began planting sugar beets, the Caribbean sugar plantations lost major revenue streams. The popularity of the new crop was devastating to them.

SUGAR FROM BEETS

The sugar beet, which has a high level of sucrose that easily crystalizes into sugar, was discovered in 1747 by German chemist Andreas Marggraf. The French initially used it to thwart the British sugar trade, but it was also more durable and easier to plant in the United States, where Louisiana had a thriving sugarcane farming industry. The sugar beet industry also became the abolitionists' alternative to sugarcane, but the sweet beet's full national acceptance would not come until after the Civil War. It thrived as settlers moved west, growing in popularity as a crop. By the 1920s, the sugar beet became an accepted sugar source.

Sugar beets were becoming known around the world. In the United Kingdom alone, sugar consumption went from two hundred thousand tons in 1843 to four hundred thousand tons in 1854. By 1882, the United Kingdom and its tea-drinking citizens consumed one million tons of sugar. Most of this sugar was from the British Sugar Islands, but they had to import some four hundred thousand tons of beet sugar from Germany, Holland, Belgium, and France. "The manufacture of beetroot sugar is entirely neglected in this country, although it has been proved that sugar beets can be grown to advantage," the *London Times* wrote in 1883.

The discovery of the sugar beet played a significant role in lowering the world's sugarcane demand and in turn hurt rum's production. USDA

The meteoric rise of the sugar beet dealt increasing blows to the Caribbean islands' industry. Within three years of Great Britain's widespread planting of sugar beets in its colonies, "Europe was flooded with beet sugar and cane sugar fell at a fearful rate. Not only was this noticeable in the wholesale and refining trades, but housekeepers found their sugars cheapened to one-half the former costs," observed the *St. Louis Post-Dispatch*. Within a decade, the world powers were planting sugar beets, and sugarcane dependence drastically dropped.

The popularity of sugar beets created one positive result for rum. Because there was less molasses, distillers used more fresh cane juice. In general, the sugar beet industry hurt cane plantations, but as a distillation base, sugar beets stood no chance against the cane. While every drop of beetroot juice can be turned into crystalized sugar, it does not yield the same type of molasses that comes from sugarcane. Whereas the British sugar islands provided the molasses to be distilled for rum, the sugar beet countries didn't know what to do with beetroot molasses. In the 1910s, George Martineau wrote in *Sugar Cane and Beet: An Object Lesson*: "In places like Jamaica and Demerara, celebrated for their rum, there is no question with the molasses, it goes to the distillery and is made into rum. The sale of rum in these countries is an important item in the account. . . . In some beetroot countries, it goes to the ordinary distillery. In Germany, it goes to special factories which extract the sugar from it by chemical processes, and actually produce white sugar as their final product."

Although a shift in molasses distillation could have occurred in the early 1900s, when beetroot was on the increase, rum continued to be created from sugarcane grown predominantly in its historic areas near the seas. During sugar beet's rise, there were reports of rum shortages.

In 1902, in a page one editorial, *The Inter Ocean* newspaper in Chicago tackled the epidemic of lost rum:

> The disappearance of rum from the general market is one of the curiosities of drinking. Half a century ago it was a standard tipple. Its admirers will tell you that it has every quality to endear. . . . Old rum drinkers will put themselves in evidence to prove that it is a wholesome drink when used with discretion. They will also tell you that there is something about it which appeals to the palate and satisfies as no other liquor does. Why, then has rum drinking passed away so largely?

The newspaper blamed the rise in taxes and whiskey's dominance for rum's disappearance but believed the strengthening temperance movement exploited the "evil reputation attached to the name of rum. . . . Rum was at the height of its popularity when the temperance movement began to be vigorous." Rum received the brunt of the early temperance attack. "The rum demon and the rum shop, and rum itself, have been made synonyms of intemperance and all its evils." No doubt, other alcoholic drinks suffered the sweeping strength of Carrie Nation and her ax-wielding Woman's Christian Temperance Union, but rum was their easiest target for several reasons.

Rum's heritage countries were islands far away from the US temperance battles, and they couldn't defend against the propaganda in the same fashion as whiskey distillers. As the bourbon distillers formed the Kentucky Distillers'

Association in 1880 to protect their interests and many distillers held prominent places in US govenment, temperance leaders pounded rum with libelous statements such as this:

> "The missionaries seek the heathen to save them from the hands of a traditional devil; the temperance reformers battle with an actual devil—Rum!—to free the victims from his grasp, and save them from the flames of an earthly hell, a hell that roars with its everlasting fires, a hell that is filled with fiends who torture alike the innocent and the guilty, who devastate the earth, who triumph in the sufferings of men, of women, of children, of babes!"
> —*The World Moves: All Goes Well* by A. Layman, 1890

Whiskey and gin faced similar attacks, but they maintained medicinal integrity. For rum, this acceptance waned, and so-called rum doctors were challenged for hurting patients. In 1910, the *Boston Medical and Surgical Journal*

Jamaican Rum

In 1907, Jamaican rum received a special designation in the United States. The Customs office issued an order to ensure that anything called "Jamaican Rum" was indeed from Jamaica. "The Board direct that rums imported from Jamaica or admitted as being of Jamaica origin, are to be entered in the accounts and on all relative documents, including permits as 'Rum from Jamaica.' Care is to be taken that this description is not applied to rum from Jamaica which has been blended with rum of other origin."

This shows the value and importance of Jamaican rum at a time when the category was losing major market share to whiskey.

In the early 1900s, the Mona Sugar Estate distillery (Jamaica) was thriving with state-of-the-art mixing cisterns and pumps. Unfortunately, the Mona Sugar Estate closed long ago. LIBRARY OF CONGRESS

1902 Volcano

Martinique is a beautiful French Caribbean island, and one that has the most sophisticated rum laws. In 1902, one of the worst natural disasters of the twentieth century occurred there. The eruption of the volcano Mount Pelée killed some thirty thousand people and destroyed fifty distilleries in Saint-Pierre. Rum was its chief export, but the islanders reportedly did not drink. They were revered as some of the finest people in the world. William A. Garesché wrote,

> No cock fighting, gambling, bull fighting or other such amusements, indulged in by some of the Latin races, were known in Martinique, and any attempt to introduce them would have been frowned on by the people, black as well as white. The island was equipped with the finest sugar factories, having all the most modern machinery to manufacture sugar and centrifuge it, separating the raw sugar from the molasses. The molasses thus obtained was then transferred to the rum distilleries, where they manufactured the finest rum in the world, all the surplus of the island being taken by the nearby West India Island, the bulk being demanded by French, both in its raw and mature condition. The town of St. Pierre manufactured the finest liquors in the world. They were shipped to France, bottled in fancy glass and reshipped to the countries abroad, labeled as "French Liqueurs." In addition to Creme de Menthe, Curaçao, and other well-known liquors, Martinique sent abroad "Parfait Amour" in English, Perfect Love—"Creme de la Vanilla," Cream of Vanilla, "Creme des Ananas," "Cream of Pineapple," and others too numerous to mention.

Firsthand accounts said that thousands of rum casks exploded and flaming rum ran down the streets and into the sea. The Saint-Pierre volcano and earthquake was an unthinkable tragedy that likely put the tariffs and the rum and whiskey legislation wars into perspective. Each of the fifty distilleries destroyed had the capacity to produce five thousand liters of rum a day. Guadalupe rum makers took on their fellow French colony's rum demands.

Initially, there were major economic consequences for sugarcane production and rum. But World War I reinvigorated Martinique's rum production, as the major distilling countries were called upon for medicinal rum. In 1914, the island's seventy-five distilleries produced 6.3 million

published a lengthy study of rabbits being injected with medicinal spirits, which compared rum, brandy, whiskey, and gin. The rabbits injected with rum died, and rum was therefore deemed "more toxic than [pure] alcohol, whisky or brandy." Meanwhile, the temperance doctors called rum prescribers "murderers."

Nonetheless, as rum's medicinal qualities lost favor, Americans loved the taste of rum, especially in cocktails.

gallons, which would be used for medicinal purposes and consumption. While that was a mere dent in the overall alcohol production the world needed, Martinique's rum was revered and preferred. A 1950s writer said that Martinique rum was the "ideal strong drink on warm days."

Today, there are seven Martinique distilleries: La Favorite, Depaz, Saint James, La Mauny, JM, Simon, and Neisson. The island's flavor profile continues to be as rich and robust as it was in the early 1900s. Thus, the island's rum heritage rebounded from the horrible tragedy.

The incident also brought forward a great deal of attention toward island rum at a time when rum was losing the battle to whiskey.

The 1902 Saint-Pierre, Martinique, volcano eruption was one of the great tragedies of the twentieth century. More than thirty thousand people died. It also de-stroyed fifty distilleries.
LIBRARY OF CONGRESS

AMERICA'S COCKTAIL SCENE

America, especially New England, regained its rum-distilling prowess in the 1910s, exporting the bulk of its rum to Africa; its future state, Hawaii, ventured into rum distilling at profitable rates. Rum was being made in Kansas, New York, North Carolina, and even Kentucky, because demand for rum was high. (Many of these distilleries made multiple spirits.) There were even rums labeled bottled-in-bond—a term revered in bourbon for being at least four years old, distilled and bottled at the one distillery, and bottled at 100 proof.

This rebound of US rum consumption can be directly tied to how rum was consumed—in punches and flips.

In George Kappeler's 1897 book *Modern American Drinks*, he suggested rum cocktails over all other spirits. Kappeler even told readers to add a dash of Jamaican rum in his Brandy Smash recipe. John William Severin Gouley, the famous dining critic, wrote in the early 1900s that rum makes the most "quarrelsome and pugnacious kind of drink." Martinique, Antigua, Santa Cruz (Saint Croix), and Jamaican rums were considered the best, he wrote, while New England rums were inferior but still better than tafia, cachaça, bess-a-besse, and chicha de caña.

Because it was so easily mixed into a cocktail, rum came under additional scrutiny. Rum punches were one of the temperance movement's greatest enemies, along with the gin cocktail and hot Tom and Jerry. According to temperance leaders, the rum punch "murders the fathers of thousands of our dear boys and girls every year in his showy saloons as well as in his dark, dirty cellars. He poisons men and women to death. He robs his victims of their money first, and then kills them afterwards. A hard-hearted demon is the demon of drink."

Rum cocktails were blamed for multiple poisoning deaths in the early 1900s, too. After two men in Iola, Kansas, were declined whiskey, they drank a concoction of bay rum, lemon extract, and ginger—then died. The sheriff did not believe it was actually rum, but because that's what the deceased had called it, he pursued all the so-called rum artists.

In the 1900s, politicians were beginning to be swayed by temperance minds, whose votes were becoming vast. And thus, they began to cease drinking in public, to the point politicians made the headlines for not accepting a rum cocktail. When Vice President Charles W. Fairbanks declined a rum cocktail in Spokane, Washington, in 1907, his lemonade preference made the front page of the *New York Times*. Of course, that's not because Fairbanks disliked rum. On the contrary, a few weeks before the *NYT* mentioned this episode, he ordered a cocktail at a fundraiser dinner for his vice-presidential campaign, causing an uproar among his supporters. A Methodist reverend outed the Fairbanks table for drinking a rum cocktail. For about a week, the papers debated whether the politician—a supposed teetotaler amassing temperance votes—had consumed a rum drink. According to the *Washington Post*, "the Fairbanks family provided for a cocktail for each of the guests, and that

Early 1900s Rum Recipes

JAMAICA RUM PUNCH

Fill a mixing glass half-full of fine ice, add 1 tablespoon of fine sugar, a little water, the juice of half a lemon, one jigger of Jamaican rum and one jigger of Irish whiskey; mix well, strain into a fancy bar-glass, trim with fruit, or leave on ice, and serve with straws.

CENTURY CLUB PUNCH

Fill a mixing glass half-full of fine ice, add 1 tablespoon of fine sugar, a little water, the juice of half a lemon, half a jigger of Jamaican rum and half a jigger of Saint Croix rum; shake well. Serve in a long, thin glass with straws, trim with fruits in season.

EGGNOG FRAPPE

Beat two eggs until light and creamy, add 2 tablespoons of fine sugar, beat again, then add half a jigger of Saint Croix rum, half a jigger of brandy, and 1 pint of cream or rich milk; mix well and freeze.

RUM DAISY

Fill a mixing glass half full of fine ice, add three dashes of gum syrup, the juice of half a lemon, three dashes of orange cordial, one jigger of rum; shake well, strain into fizz-glass, fill with siphon seltzer.

BISHOP

Fill a long, thin punch glass half-full of fine ice, the juice of a quarter of a lemon, the juice of half an orange, one dash of Jamaica rum, two jiggers of Burgundy, 1 tablespoon of fine sugar. Mix well, fill the glass with seltzer, ornament with fruit. Serve with straws.

SOURCE: GEORGE J. KAPPELER, 1895

the order was given four days before the President was expected to arrive; that at the last moment Mrs. Fairbanks discovered that the cocktails had been overlooked, and she appealed to Mayor Bookwalter [of Indianapolis], whose automobile was standing in the yard, to go to the Columbia Club." And so, for nearly a month, professional journalists investigated Fairbanks's alleged consumption of a rum cocktail.

In a similar story, in August 1919, just months before the United States enacted Prohibition, the Prince of Wales—later Edward VIII, King of England—made international news when he bottoms-upped a rum punch at the Studley Quoit Club in Halifax, Canada. It was called the "most cheerful" moment of his time in Canada.

But this would be one of rum's final positive news stories in 1919. Prohibition talks dominated the media, and change was coming. Nonetheless, for the drinking population, nothing was quite as appealing as the rum punch. Liquor stores started selling rum punch by the bottle for the same price as a bottle of bourbon—$1.

Unfortunately, dry consumers owned the White House and Congress at that time. The Volstead Act went into law, prohibiting the manufacturing and sale of alcohol from 1920 to 1933. Funny thing is, rum was never more popular than after it was banned.

Like the pirates before them, the Prohibition-era rumrunners worked with rum dealers in the Caribbean to resell without government approval. They picked up rum from the islands and sold them to the American bootleggers at ports—most notably in New Orleans or Miami. Unlike the notorious mobsters born in Prohibition, rumrunners were considered heroes to many. Although illegally selling to unsavory types off American shores, they were providing economic relief to financially depressed islands. Renowned US journalist Jack Lait called rumrunners the "realtors" of kindness, even if they illegally transported intoxicants, carried guns, were arrested, and engaged in violent conflict with authorities.

The cat-and-mouse game between rumrunners and revenue agents catapulted law enforcement careers and contributed to mafia empires. Al Capone ran Cuban rum through Florida and was in Miami during the infamous Saint Valentine's Day Massacre in 1929.

Rumrunners also had a way of bribing officials into giving them safe harbor into the United States. Occasionally, these bribes were uncovered—such as in the 1924 case of New York politician Daniel J. Shields's speakeasy getting busted, in which leading agents were discovered to have been assisting in various rum-running activities.

The password-protected speakeasies also kept rum's taste and mixability alive, serving rum punches, flips, sours—and new cocktails, such as the El Presidente. Rum was so popular in the speakeasy that true rum was hard to come by. Many illegal bars purchased spirits that the seller called rum, but which was actually poison liquor, likely made in somebody's basement, bathtub, or in the woods under the cover of night. And of course, there were those entrepreneurial bootleggers offering so-called rum for around thirteen cents a half pint. Only, it wasn't rum at all: according to one Philadelphia bust, cheap rum was 80 percent water and only 20 percent spirit.

Unless you knew the rum was coming from a reliable rumrunner, such as Bill Mc-Coy, and delivered by a trusted bootlegger, such as George Remus, you could not trust that the rum you were drinking in the 1920s was actually rum. Throughout Prohibition, gangs were outed for selling "fake rum" and their trials offered a glimpse into how society vilified phony rum versus the good stuff. Fake rum was often poisonous and connected to many deaths. Doctors and druggists were fake rum's leading distributors, often working

Rum is the lead mixer in many cocktails thanks to its forward flavor profile and tasty combination potential. But leading up to Prohibition, the rum cocktail was one of the primary enemies of temperance. As Prohibition was enacted, cartoonists began depicting rum as a drink for demons. More so than other spirits, rum was connected to evil doings. LIBRARY OF CONGRESS

together to prescribe fake rum instead of bonded medicinal whiskey. In 1925, 787 New York medical professionals were caught prescribing more than one million fake rums and counterfeit whiskeys to patients. It was a national epidemic.

After Prohibition ended in 1933, rum's biggest story was Bacardi's exile from Cuba when Fidel Castro confiscated the country's rum distilleries in 1960. The family set up facilities in Puerto Rico (where it is now headquartered), Mexico, Brazil, the Bahamas, and the Canary Islands, earning far more than would have been possible under Castro's regime had he allowed them to stay. (The Bacardi history is far too complex for this chapter to fully discuss. For more,

Bill McCoy became a famous rumrunner during Prohibition. If rum or whiskey came from his ship, you knew it was the real McCoy.

REAL MCCOY SPIRITS CO.

read Tom Gjelten's *Bacardi and the Long Fight for Cuba: The Biography of a Cause*.)

In addition to nudging Bacardi into changing homes, the United States greatly interfered with the rum business in the twentieth century.

In 1917, the US government purchased three Caribbean islands from Denmark: Saint Thomas, Saint Croix, and Saint John Island, together known as the Virgin Islands. Rum was a centerpiece for all three, and distillers earned earmarked tax revenue for their respective islands. That same year, Congress passed the Jones Act of 1917, which stipulated for the existing territory of Puerto Rico, "providing that hereafter all taxes collected under the internal revenue laws of the United States on articles produced in Porto Rico [*sic*] and transported to the United States, or consumed in the island shall be covered over into the treasury of Porto Rico [*sic*]."

But for the Virgin Island distilleries, the government kept a share, including the product known as "Government House Rum." Perhaps because they were contributing to US revenues and therefore felt entitled, the island operators consistently requested additional funds to maintain rum distilleries. In 1948, the islands requested $7,700,000 from Congress to renovate one of the rum distilleries. Prior to this request, the government pumped $10,000,000 into the island.

The steady requests for money were eventually answered. In 1954, Congress created the same cover-over program it did for Puerto Rico nearly forty years earlier. The Virgin Islands' governments now received all taxes collected on rum distilleries there, through the Revised Organic Act of 1954:

There shall be transferred and paid over to the government of the Virgin Islands from the amounts so determined a sum equal to the total amount of revenue collected by the government of the Virgin Islands during the fiscal year, as certified by the Government Comptroller of the Virgin Islands. The money so transferred and paid over shall constitute a separate fund in the treasury of the Virgin Islands and may be expended as the legislature may determine.

In 1984, the cover-over rum tax was capped at $10.50, and the Virgin Islands and Puerto Rico introduced subsidies to support rum production. Since then, both Puerto Rico and the Virgin Islands keep the excise taxes, while US taxpayers assist in paying for the production, marketing, and employee salaries.

More than twenty years later, the US government subsidized the world's largest spirits company, Diageo, to open the Captain Morgan distillery on the United States Virgin Islands. Diageo will receive nearly $3 billion over thirty years, including a $165 million distillery and payments to keep the cost of molasses low. If you've ever wondered why there

Tiki Drinks

The tiki drink is all the rage today, and it all began just after Prohibition.

In 1934, Don the Beachcomber, owner of a Hollywood-area Polynesian bar and restaurant, began featuring delicious rum punches that boasted flaming torches, furniture, flowers, and colorful accessories. A few years later, Trader Vic adopted a similar setup in Oakland.

Their drinks would shine at the 1939 Golden Gate International Exposition, which celebrated US Polynesian culture. As Trader Vic's became a chain, drinks such as the mai tai became beloved and much sought after. (Read more about cocktails in the cocktail section.)

Today, tiki bars still dominate the culture for Hawaiian shirt wearers. In 2005, the Fraternal Order of the Moai Foundation formed a 501(c)(3) charity with nine chapters across the United States. It celebrates the tiki culture that believes rum to be the world's most enjoyable spirit.

In 1934, Don the Beachcomber opened a Polynesian bar in Hollywood, jumpstarting the zeitgeist of tiki culture. Drinks would never be the same.

While the travel brochures depict the Caribbean as bright and sunny, it rains 127 days a year in Antigua and 208 days in Vieux Fort. Of course, the rain is good for thirsty sugarcane. In Barbados—just across the street in this photo—grow Mount Gay's freshly planted sugarcane fields.

are so many Captain Morgan commercials, it is because the company spends about 35 percent of this subsidy on advertising. It also receives a 90 percent income-tax break, property tax exemptions, and 47.5 percent of all tax revenue collected on Captain Morgan. Several estimates indicate that Diageo's net cost to create Captain Morgan is zero—an amazing business model. For Diageo shareholders, who wouldn't want this sweet deal?

But the cover-over naysayers believe "the unintended consequences of the cover-over program have led both Puerto Rico and the US Virgin Islands to manipulate their economies to maximize federal subsidies. The ensuing subsidies race distorts the economy, creates perverse incentives, and destabilizes local government," wrote Adam Michel for the Barbados newspaper *Nation News*.

An argument also can be made that these subsidies created the "rum and Coke" and the frozen daiquiri—two drinks fueled by industrialized plants pumping out subsidized rum.

Smaller-scale distillers simply cannot compete with Bacardi or Cruzan on an international scale, but nevertheless, many smaller distillers, including Mount Gay and Appleton, never stopped distilling and have received investments from outsiders to bolster capacity and market their products. Today, many rums are made exactly the way they were in the 1800s—and it all starts with sugarcane.

CHAPTER 2

PRODUCTION

RUM BEGINS IN THE SUGARCANE FIELDS in the Caribbean islands, Central America, South America, Louisiana, and other climates with warm growing seasons. This includes even the US state of Georgia, where 140 acres of sugarcane rise up from sandy loam soil just a few miles from former US President Jimmy Carter's childhood home.

In Richland, Georgia, Erik and Karin Vonk planted sugarcane on an estate with a well running deep into an underground river. In the field four hundred feet above sea level, flowing with weeds and bordered by pine trees, the Vonks hand-pull every weed and irrigate the sandy loam soil weekly, sometimes daily. "Sugarcane is labor intensive," says Vonk, adding that this is the reason why slavery was connected to sugarcane—it can't prosper without human toil. It's also becoming less economical for the rum

Sugarcane grows in humid climates and features many breeds. This cane grows in the St. Nicholas Abbey fields in Barbados.

heritage countries. In Barbados, arguably the home of this beautiful spirit, commercial development signs stand in once-thriving sugarcane fields. This has forced Mount Gay and Foursquare to import molasses and cease exclusive use of Barbados-based cane. "Sugarcane and other agriculture is just not as profitable as a golf course or condo development," says Simon Warren, manager of St. Nicholas Abbey, which grows some 240 acres of cane in Barbados.

At many Caribbean distilleries, you'll find sugarcane presses that appear to be more relics than working machinery, such as this beautiful press at St. Nicholas Abbey in Barbados.

According to international sugarcane firm Netafim, sugarcane requires significant moisture, optimum temperatures between 30 and 38 degrees Celsius for germination, humidity between 45 and 65 percent, ten to fourteen hours of sunlight per day, and a sandy loam soil with a decent pH level.

Due to the sugarcane demands from ethanol plants and food manufacturers, scientists are beginning to implement genetically modified sugarcane, mostly found in the United States and Brazil. More than half of the world's cane-based sugar is derived from the species *Saccharum officinarum*. Other species include *Saccharum barberi*, *Saccharum sinensis*, *Saccharum spontaneum*, and *Saccharum robustum*, but within these species are varieties that are developed to grow in different soils and rainfall amounts. In Barbados, for example, the Barbados Cane Industry Corporation maintains more than thirty cane varieties that can grow in shallow or deep soils with low to high rainfall. Sometimes the variety known as B79474 grows next to B82238, and the distillery never even knows. This amalgamation makes it more difficult for distillers to discern their desired sugarcane source.

The sugarcane is harvested several times a year in different regions. It's then pressed using any number of devices—from at-home sugarcane presses available online for $400 to vintage hand-crank juicers. Whether done by crank or industrial presser, the goal is to separate the juice from the pulp to ensure it contains maximum sucrose, a carbohydrate in fruits and vegetables. Sucrose is also found in grains and grapes, which is suitable for making respectable whiskey and brandy, but rum requires more sucrose than is contained by other sources used for distilled spirits, such as corn, rye, Airén grapes, and apples.

Once the cane is juiced, the liquid is filtered through a cloth and then cooked. As the liquid heats, the water evaporates and sugar crystalizes. During this boiling process, a thick syrup—molasses—is left behind after the sugar crystals are extracted. The sugar crystals, with additional processing, will become raw sugar. The quality of the molasses used for rum varies based on sugar extraction, cane quality, and the number of boils it has undergone. After one boil, there's more sweetness to the molasses. The second boil creates molasses that is darker and has less sugar. After three boils, the substance contains the least amount of sweetness and is commonly referred to as "blackstrap molasses." Blackstrap molasses was also sold as treacle—a sweetener for home use.

While molasses is the most common sugarcane substance used for rum, it's not the only one. One of the more common sugarcane-based substances is cane syrup, widely used for cooking in prominent sugarcane areas.

To create cane syrup, the cane juice is boiled in a kettle at a lower temperature than when refining molasses until it foams. The foam is skimmed and filtered for impurities until enough water evaporates to leave a syrup that is almost golden in color. For roughly every ten gallons of cane juice, there is one gallon of syrup created. In Guatemala, rum must come from fermented virgin sugarcane honey—filtered sugarcane juice that has been boiled until the syrup is around 70 percent sugar.

Cane juice itself is about 14 percent sucrose. The Martinique and Guadaloupe producers distill freshly pressed cane juice, which is the closest in flavor to the rawness of sugarcane. This style is rare in the grand scheme of rum and is referred to as "rhum agricole" instead of rum.

The rum base is mostly molasses, a byproduct of sugar manufacturing. Paradoxically, the worse the sugar manufacturer, the better the molasses they produce. "The major American sugar houses have horrible molasses, because their plants are so efficient," said Andrew Hassell, managing director of the West Indies Rum Distillery. "They also use a lot chemicals [in the sugarcane] and that can destroy the yeast."

The cane juice and syrup-based distillers swear by their methods, as is the case with Erik Vonk, who insists that molasses is a downgrade from cane syrup and regards molasses as "waste." Meanwhile, molasses distillers say molasses offers a touch more consistency, is less expensive, is more widely available, and has more concentrated flavor. In truth, the layperson may not be able to discern the taste profile difference between cane syrup and molasses.

Nonetheless, many rum distillers purchase molasses from a broker, who sources the black tarry substance from a number of islands and countries. This is another reason why distillers could never really know their sugarcane species—it's sourced from all over the world.

Other Cane Spirits

Caribbean rum production methods and traditions set the standard for cane-based distillation. But other sugarcane spirits have their own heritage and command unique styles, with names other than "rum."

Other cane-based spirits, cachaça and Batavia arrack, are slightly different from rum and have geographical identities. Batavia arrack is made in Indonesia from molasses, rice, and botanicals. *Arrack* is a common term for distilled spirits, especially in Arabic countries, and *Batavia*, present-day Jakarta, was the Dutch capital of the East Indies. So, when Batavia arrack was created in the 1600s, it was named after the Dutch city. The Dutch were rum drinkers and influencers, but the Indonesian people influenced the spirit with their rice and botanicals. Early American newspapers recognized Batavia arrack as unique and different from rum, with the Philadelphia newspaper the *Independent Gazetteer* referring to it as "excellent" and "old" in 1787. Batavia arrack also comes in many older expressions, which has led to quite the following of enthusiasts, some of whom believe the category is better than rum.

Cachaça is not rum, but it shares many similarities, including its distilled fresh sugarcane juice. Brazilians and many rum makers prefer to keep them separated.

Meanwhile, cachaça (pronounced *kha-shah-sah*) has international geographical protection since it can only be made in Brazil. Cachaça producers do not care for being called rum, and rum producers reciprocate the feeling. Cachaça consists of fermented fresh sugarcane juice distilled to no higher than 54 percent ABV, and bottled between 38 percent and 48 percent ABV at 20 degrees Celsius. Some is unaged, but the aged products are stored in wood of unrestricted origin. Wood containers are up to seven hundred liters. "Aged" cachaça is 50 percent aged for a period of not less than one year, "premium" 100 percent is aged for a period of not less than one year, and "extra premium" 100 percent is aged for at least three years. Cachaça cannot have detectable sugar above six grams per liter.

In 2008, Leblon Cachaça pursued a "rum versus cachaça" campaign in which they suggested that it was superior to rum. In the campaign, Lablon stated, "So why then the rum question? According to US law, any spirit derived from sugar cane must be labeled as a rum—in Cachaça's case, 'Brazilian rum.' This nomenclature has been in dispute for some time, with proposals to separate Cachaça into its own 'class,' like tequila, or into an 'appellation' within a broader class, like cognac and champagne. With the increasing popularity of Cachaça, more and more people are asking for the distinction, especially since the cultural and sensorial differences between rum and Cachaça are so significant."

South Africa also produces a so-called cane spirit that consists of fermented molasses that has been column distilled; South America, especially Colombia, is known for its *aguardiente*, a general term for spirits that often, but not always, means distilled molasses with a mixture of fruits or vegetables.

In the United States, moonshiners and some craft distillers make spirit from sugar. These are not considered rum; however, because the United States has already allowed sugar-beet and molasses rums, who knows—maybe one day sugar 'shine will be rum according to US legal standards.

West Indies Rum Distillery was once the go-to facility for custom distillation for Caribbean rums. But recent political moves in the United States have made it more difficult for the distillery to compete against subsidized rum manufacturers.

No matter the source, the distillers test it for Brix—the percentage of sugar by weight in a solution. According to the yeast and fermentation specialist White Labs, molasses weight is also an important indicator of quality because handling and storage can reduce volume and reduce sugar content. Bulk molasses should be stored around 113 degrees Fahrenheit, but not all molasses comes with temperature reports, so distillers must test its weight.

Next, water and yeast may be added to start fermentation, or water and yeast naturally invade the material and natural fermentation begins. Both water and yeast significantly impact the rum's final flavor profile.

Many rum distillers use water filtered by reverse osmosis, a process that removes dissolved inorganic solids through a semipermeable membrane. Some, such as Mount Gay, have access to their own onsite wells and draw straight from underground aquifers and rivers. Much like American whiskey, limestone-filtered water assists many rum producers, including Caribbean distillers. Simply put, as with any distilled spirit, the more naturally filtered the water, the better the distillate.

But as Plantation's Alexandre Gabriel says, water's importance is both romantic and technical:

> Romantic story-telling makes a whole fuss about the source the water comes from. . . . The technical fact is that, while water is very important for spirits, the most important thing is to have access to really pure and non-mineral water. A heavy "mineral charged" water will flatten and therefore destroy the taste. This is why, most serious spirit producers in the past were relying on distilled water and now on osmosis filtration. Once you have pure water, the most important thing is how you use it. Water should never be integrated too fast to a spirit. It should always be a progressive reduction so as not to shock irreparably the rum.

Of course, there's a difference between water used in fermentation and water used in spirit reduction. At the Hampden Distillery in Jamaica, for example, the natural spring water provides a vital microbiological flora for fermentation. On the other hand, Foursquare's Richard Seale says that water for reduction must be pure: "The less pure, the more the slowly it must be added to avoid the shock."

As for yeast, rum distillers face greater challenges than whiskey or brandy distillers. As White Labs notes, it's slightly more complicated than simply adding yeast, a living organism, and allowing it to feed upon sugars to create alcohol. The fermentation consultant company says, "Although abundant in fermentable sugars, any type of molasses or pure sugar fermentation medium is lacking in essential nutrients required by the yeast for a healthy metabolism. It does, however, have a healthy population of bacteria and or wild yeast that can take over fermentation, producing excess amounts of acetic and butyric acids which are toxic to yeast."

Some distillers will add an acid or an enzyme to control bacterial infestations. The yeast added to the fermentation process can include dried, propagated, or wild yeast.

Once the yeast is added, fermentation temperatures are essential. Caribbean fermentation temperatures can reach 90 degrees Fahrenheit, but the lower temperatures (75 to 80 degrees) achieve better alcohol yields, White Labs suggests. "Temperature control is very necessary, as final fermentation temperatures are a function of the sugar concentration and ambient temperatures, which are in the range of 25 to 32°C," writes Andrew G. H. Lea, author of *Fermented Beverage*

Rum destinations allow for vacation comforts, beaches, sailboat cruises, and long walks on the beach. This view is from the Hilton Barbados.

Production. "Thus, fermentation temperatures are maintained at 30 to 33°C. Cooling is performed by external heat exchangers, internal cooling coils, or water jackets . . . Molasses fermentations proceed at a very high rate—within twenty-four hours, fully attenuated wash is produced, yielding 5 to 7 percent alcohol by volume."

For many, the act of fermentation dominates the end flavor. In 1945, legendary rum author Rafael Arroyo wrote that it was the most important step to rum making, adding that the quality "depends almost entirely on the quantity and quality of the congener produced by sugarcane product's alcoholic fermentation."

Rum's fermentation protocol is more vast and complex than most spirits because distillers' base greatly varies. Their base includes sugarcane juice, fresh sugarcane juice, molasses, and cane syrup. All require their own expertise to ferment. This is fermenting sugarcane syrup at Richland Rum in Richland, Virginia.

In recent years, the term *congener* has come to be associated with hangovers, with studies indicating that the more congeners that are present, the greater the hangover. But let's face it— you drink too much, you get a hangover. From a flavor perspective, congeners are the compounds that create the esters, lactones, and hydroxyl compounds. Achieving the coveted esters in fermentation is what separates good rum from great rum, and the distillation and maturation is what moves great rum into the discussion on exceptional rums.

In the most basic sense, distillation involves heating the fermented liquid in a still so that the ethanol (the alcohol) is separated from water and turned into vapor, which contains more alcohol than the fermented wash. The vapor is then condensed and collected. One of the better explanations, written for the home distiller audience, comes from New Zealand chemist and distiller Tony Ackland:

> We can then make the vapor more pure by letting it be "stripped" of its water content by passing it up through a packed column which has some condensed vapor running back down through it as liquid. When the two pass each other, the vapor will absorb alcohol from the falling liquid, and the liquid will take some of the water from the vapor. Distilling doesn't "make" the alcohol, nor turn some of it "bad," or into something that will blind you; it's only collecting the alcohol that was made during fermentation.

Of course, rum distillation is much more complicated than simply turning wash—the term used for distiller's beer—into spirit. This category has incredible distillation diversity, which leads to various styles and rum-making techniques.

Rum distillation includes pot and column distillation. After it's distilled, many brands will blend the pot and column to create their preferred flavor profile. From left to right are the column still at West Indies, the pot stills at Mount Gay, and the pot still at Foursquare. All are in Barbados.

Rum can enjoy any of several types of distillation processes: single-column distillation, single-pot, multicolumn distillation, and double-pot distillation, among others.

The continuous-column stills are easy to operate, can be run constantly, and are fundamentally more efficient than pot stills. So, if you're running a business with consistency and profits in mind, a column still sounds nice. Many pure column-still rums are also quite lovely, but some columns are better than others for achieving flavor.

Often romanticized, pot stills require more hands-on work, including cleaning and control measures, than continuous stills. After the fermented liquid is pumped into the pot vessel, it's heated and the spirit is collected in a second vessel as "low wines," which are then distilled into "high wines." The distiller must either make cuts of the spirit or high wines, keeping the middle part of the run, or distill it again. Pot stills come off at lower proof and typically allow for more nuances in the spirit, although this isn't always the case.

Many call the column-made rums the lighter styles, while the pot-still rums are known as heavy styles.

For many, rum's greatest styles are the blends of pot and column. "Rum is so unique because you see both pot and column stills in traditional distilleries. Rum is the only category outside of Scotland that blends pot and column," says Foursquare's Seale.

Foursquare uses the modern version of a Coffey continuous still, which was built in 1996. There's a mash column and a stripping column that rectifies the spirit. Foursquare's pot still is a classic Caribbean double-retort pot that Seale says is more high tech than European pot stills because "it can do everything in one go and we can take smaller hearts"—the core section of the spirit that yields the majority of the flavor.

> The pot still is a batch still and a column still is a continuous still; that is the fundamental difference. It is not pot vs. column, it is batch vs. continuous. The difference between the two then has little to do with column and plates. You can make a column still with no plates, but it would be tough. When you have a pot still, the gooseneck is the plate. When you put plates inside, you are increasing liquid vapor contact. In the pot, the gooseneck is the plate ... and the atmosphere is the cooling.

In the nineteenth century, many Caribbean pot stills were outfitted with a rectifying section, but the pot still remains a batch process.

After distillation, the spirit is either cut with water and bottled; blended with the pot and column distillates, unaged, and bottled; adulterated with additives to the brand's specifications and bottled; or put into a barrel. If it's unaged, its story then stops. You buy the unaged rum, mix it, or drink it straight; the rum's flavor journey is completed and can only be enhanced by you or the bartender. If it's aged, the flavor profile begins to take off.

Rum distillers purchase barrels from Kentucky and Tennessee whiskey distillers, who are bound by regulation to use barrels only once for bourbon and Tennessee whiskey. The French distillers use French oak almost exclusively. After the barrels are dumped, they are sent to the rum producers via boat, rail, or truck, depending on the distiller's location.

Typically, used bourbon barrels are made of American white oak, which comprises 45 percent cellulose, 25 percent lignin, 22 percent hemicellulose, and 0.8 to 10 percent oak tannins. The key flavor creators are lignin and hemicellulose. By law, bourbon barrels must be charred—a practice involving pure flame engulfing the wood for anywhere from fifteen to ninety seconds. The most common char is a char No. 4, which is fifty-five seconds of pure flame. Charring

Aged rum is typically stored in used bourbon barrels, which are American oak. Some rum is finished in additional barrels, such as cognac, Madeira, port, and sherry. While in the wood, the rum interacts with wood sugars that give rum much of its flavor and aroma. Pictured are the warehouses and barrels of Mount Gay.

caramelizes the wood sugars (the lignin and hemicellulose), bringing out flavors of caramel, spice, smoke, coconut, mocha, and vanilla in the wood. The wood gives bourbon its color, aroma, and most of its flavor, but the whiskey also strips out some of the flavor.

For every year bourbon sits in a Kentucky warehouse, it penetrates deeper into the wood and extracts more wood sugars, leaving fewer flavors behind. For this reason, many rum distillers refuse to buy used barrels that have aged bourbon for more than twelve years—there's just no flavor left in the barrel, according to some. Other distillers, though, love a "worn-out" barrel, suggesting that exotic flavors remain in the cask for up to twenty-five years of bourbon aging.

No matter how long it aged bourbon, the most crucial phase for a barrel that will later be used for rum is after it's dumped. If it's dumped then sits outside for a week, the wood can warp and fall victim to the elements. Worms, birds, rain, snow, wind, and even termites can destroy the barrel. Appleton ensures that its barrel partner empties and ships barrels immediately to be refilled with Jamaican rum. "Poor quality barrels puts out bad odors and isn't palatable," says Joy Spence, master blender for Appleton.

Some rum distillers rechar barrels after receipt to pull out the remaining flavors in the wood. According to the world's largest cooperage, the Independent Stave Company, the barrel recharring increases the available wood sugars, but not by much. "All of our studies show that the hemicellulose breakdown products (including wood sugars) are the first to be extracted from the wood. Next is vanillin and then tannin," says Brad Boswell, owner of Independent Stave. "When I think of recharring, I primarily think of squeezing a little more lignin breakdown products (vanillin) out of the barrel."

From here, the barrels are filled and begin to age the rum. In the Caribbean, the ullage rate—the "angel's share" that evaporates—is about 6 to 12 percent per year. In the United States, it's 3 to 5 percent, while in Venezuela, ullage is as high as 15 percent per year. Essentially, the hotter and more humid the climate, and the higher the elevation, the more spirit will evaporate from the barrel.

Many rum producers make up for the angel's share by refilling their barrels or topping them off with barrels distilled on the same date. In Venezuela, though, this is prohibited.

At Appleton, the Jamaican distillery executes a refilling regime every three years, in which they line up barrels identical in age and extract rum from one barrel to fill up the rest. Spence says the goal is to maintain little headspace in the barrel and minimize loss.

The barrels age standing upright or lying horizontal inside warehouses. All distillers set a lifespan for their barrels. Mount Gay uses a barrel three times before processing it out of the distillery, while others give the barrels up to thirty years and assess them as needed.

Necessity drives the barrel's longevity. When bourbon is popular, rum distillers struggle to purchase used barrels cost effectively, competing against other spirits producers, winemakers, brewers, and even Tabasco manufacturers.

Barrel-Entry Proof

If rum distillers plan to age their spirit, the next move off the still affects its future flavor. The wood barrel contains various compounds, such as lignin, that transfer to the spirit to change its color and give a good chunk of the final flavor.

Each distiller makes a decision on the proof level based on economics and flavor profile. Some place it straight in the barrel from the still, while others cut it with water before placing it in the barrel. At this point, the actual proof is called "barrel-entry proof." In theory, barrel-entry proof makes a huge impact on the final flavor profile.

In the 1970s, scientists studied the barrel-entry proof of whiskey in new charred-oak barrels. They measured color and congener levels of twelve-year-old whiskey that had gone into the barrel at 109 and 155 proof. The results showed that higher entry-level proofs resulted in a decrease in flavor after twelve years. The additional water makes the spirit more soluble in the wood and, theoretically, less harsh.

Since American whiskey traditionally goes into new charred oak, there are more wood sugars for the spirit to extract. Rum, however, typically goes into used barrels (with a few exceptions, such as Richland Rum), and therefore the barrel-entry proof doesn't have the same impact as it does for whiskey.

With that said, as you'll see in the production notes, the brand barrel-entry proofs for rums vary greatly. Your own organoleptic comparison of the rums outlined in this book might offer a personal study to determine if barrel-entry proofs matter to you.

Barrel-entry proof is the alcohol strength at which rum enters the barrel. When it comes off the still, distillers add water, and this strength could influence the rum's flavor.

Of course, bourbon barrels are not the only casks employed in rum production, though they are the most common. Many rum distillers employ port, calvados, cognac, sherry, and other barrels. But the bulk of rum is aged in used bourbon barrels.

When the aging process is completed, some rum distillers move to another flavor measure—blending.

Rectifier Recipe for Rum

In the 1800s, a rectifier looking to make more money off the name *rum* without buying barrels from the West Indies would take inferior New England rum and mix it with other ingredients and coloring. An 1800s-era rectified rum might be concocted like this:

1 barrel New England rum
40 gallons neutral grain spirits
20 gallons prune juice

Today, rum manufacturers are not using the same methods as the 1800s-era rum rectifiers, who often colored neutral grain spirits and called it rum. But modern rum additives may well include ones similar to those used in the 1800s, such as muscat and port. And while many people find additive-laden rums offensive, the category exists and represents much of what's on the shelf.

If a rum is not sent to the additive station, coloring is often added, and it's then bottled. Unlike wine, rum and other spirits do not "age" while in the bottle. However, corks can allow evaporation to occur, and this impacts the flavor. Theoretically, you could purchase rum from the 1940s and it will taste the same as the day it was bottled. But it's also likely the cork didn't hold up during this seventy-year period, and the rum will have become oxidized.

Every production method greatly impacts the flavor, but none are more polarizing than the use of sugar.

Some rum makers sweeten their spirit prior to bottling, a method widely unwelcomed by many Caribbean distillers. Some main brands have had as much as sixty grams of recorded sugar per liter. These flavors are typically created in a lab.

"Creating a new rum blend is both science and art. Before I start, I have an overall vision of what I want—do I want to make a rum that is going to be great for making cocktails, or is it a sipping rum?" Spence says. "Once I know what type of blend I want to create, I then look at what kind of flavor profile am I looking for—for instance, do I want a rum that has a lot of oak notes in it, or am I looking for something that has more spice notes. After that I go to work—experimenting with different rums of varying styles, types and ages—seeing how the different marques of rum interact with each other and how they influence the overall profile of the blend. When I get the combinations right and the blend is what I first envisioned, then my work is done."

Others add additional spirit, sugar, honey, juice, wine, or even oak chips to obtain more flavor. Rum producers using additives are essentially practicing similar 1800s-era rectification techniques, but for different reasons. Back then, they were attempting to mimic rum—the spirits were labeled, or at least known as, *rectified rum*. These rectifiers added brandy, whiskey, prune juice, wine, and numerous other products to create a product that could pass off as rum. But the connoisseurs of the day recognized this additive method and publicly denigrated the spirit. *Collier's Cyclopedia of Commercial and Social Information*, 1886, defined rum as "A well-known spirituous liquor made in the West Indies from the sugar-cane. . . The rum which is of a brownish, transparent color, of a smooth oily taste, of a strong body and consistence, of a good age, and well kept, is the best. That of a clear, limpid color, and hot pungent taste, is either too new, or dashed with other spirits. . . " In fact, Joseph Fleishman wrote in *The Art of Blending and Compounding Liquors and Wines* that "the domestic brands of rum are generally cut 50 percent with spirits, reducing their cost to $1.30 per gallon."

Tips for Finding the Unsugared

In Appendix A (page 199), you'll see a more detailed report of which distillers use additives and which do not. Here are a few tips if you do not want rum that has been sugared:

- Barbados: Bajan laws forbid additives in its rum for products bottled there. However, if it's purchased in bulk and bottled in another country, sugar may have been added.
- South America: Traditionally, South American rum has added flavor and up to 40 grams of sugar. If you're looking for non-enhanced spirit, perhaps avoid South America.
- Jamaica: Jamaican rum is not allowed to have sugar added.
- Bottled-in-Bond: This American label regulation is rare, but it means the rum is at least four years old, was made in one distilling season at one distillery, and is not adulterated. Only US rums can have this label.

The following brands not only refrain from including additives, but they vocally express their disdain for the process: Appleton Estate, Foursquare, Mount Gay, St. Lucia Distillers, and Barbancourt are just a few brands that do not add sugar.

SUGARING

After the blending or additive methods, the rum is filtered and, typically, color is added. The darker rum is, the more color has been added. Hence, dark rum usually contains significant coloring. The food coloring is (relatively) innocuous in taste and aroma. After coloring, it may be bottled—or first, the brand adds sugar, wine, or another spirit.

If you ever find yourself eager to learn who's packing sugar, visit the Swedish government website, www.systembolaget.se. In addition to adding sugar, brands will add honey, wine, and other spirits to sweeten the end product.

Among those using sugar, only a handful talk about it—Diplomático is one of those. Diplomático says that champagne inspired the Venezuelan rum maker's use of sugar. Tito Cordero, the master distiller of Diplomático, says his rum combines aged heavy rums and Venezuelan refined sugar and is aged in oak barrels for a few additional months. Another distiller, Opthimus, adds Pedro Ximénez wine at 17 percent ABV, plus caramel, vanilla, muscat, and water, before the rum is bottled. Others are known to add glycerol, sherry, artificial flavors, honey, and syrup to their rum, giving many the perception that rum is sweet even though there is no label disclosure. These methods were common in the late 1800s by wholesalers. One "rum essence" recipe, "A Treatise on Beverages," written in 1888, states, "The addition of some prune juice (one gallon) and five to ten gallons of genuine rum to the imitation of twenty-five gallons, gives a higher grade of rum."

Back then, however, the marketplace rewarded those regions making genuine rum, such as Jamaica and Martinique. One would be hard-pressed to find a late-1800s rum aficionado who'd select a prune-juice-laden rum over Jamaican rum. Today, however, it's just the opposite. Millions of consumers expect rum to be sweet.

Recently, this author held a rum tasting with professed rum fanatics. "Oh, we love rum, everything about it!" I then conducted an experiment with them, setting out twelve rums to be tasted—six with additives, six without. Unanimously, the small focus group picked the "sweeter rums." They found the non-additive rums to "not be very smooth," as one taster said. These were not connoisseurs, but everyday people who like the occasional drink—the average consumer.

Although this offers only a micro look into the US consumer base, this study reveals the preference for sweetness in US consumers, who love sugar. This sugared market has led to cotton-candy vodka, honey whiskey, and sweetened red wines that represent some of the fastest-growing categories in adult beverages. Across the board, critics tend to reject mainstream flavor preferences and applaud the unadulterated beverages. But there's no denying it: sweet sells.

Producers are also fortunate that US regulations allow them to bottle sweetened rum without disclosure. Both the Swedish and Finnish governments test rum for sugar content. (See sidebar on page 72.)

Which is better? If you have a sweet tooth, you might actually enjoy the sugared-up rums, although some unadulterated rums, such as Appleton's blends, can still be sweet enough to satisfy your sweet tooth. However, if you come from the whiskey clans, you may desire your rums untouched and with flavor originating from cane, fermentation, distillation, and maturation.

In the end, nonadditive rums have the advantage over sugared rum in the eyes of the connoisseur. We like tasting the raw material and nuance, and sugar masks these lovely characteristics. But there are exceptions to the rule, and Peru's Cartavio is one of them. Cartavio XO captured Best Rum at the San Francisco World Spirits Competition and the New York World Wine and Spirits Competition. Making rum since 1926, the Peruvian distillery doesn't hide its sweetness. In fact, master blender Federico Schulz counters, "Rum companies have many different ways to make their products, not to mask the product but to differentiate them. For example, some treat their alcohol with carbon before aging and some after aging. Some people add sugars and/or concentrates of fruits, it all depends on the company and . . . we have to respect each company's methods."

While many brands add sugaring to sweeten their rum, flavored rum and "liqueurs" are categories all their own. Malibu Pineapple Upside Down Cake is uniquely labeled "Caribbean Rum with Coconut Liqueur, Certified Color and Caramel added."

Sugared

On its website Systembolaget.se, the Swedish government discloses the additive readings from its tests. These tests are for the Swedish market and are only representative of the bottlings for Sweden and may not be the same as the readings for rum bottled in other markets. But they provide public information on who adds sugar and how much.

Here are just a few. (The appendix on page 199 also identifies who adds sugar, but in less detail than offered here.)

- Angostura 1919, 15 grams per liter
- Diplomático Reserva Exclusiva 12 Años, 41 grams per liter
- El Dorado 15 Years, 31 grams per liter
- Negrita Dark, fewer than 3 grams per liter
- Ron Zacapa Gran Reserva, 41 grams per liter
- Plantation XO 20th Anniversary, 29 grams per liter
- Ron Zacapa XO, 26 grams per liter
- Bacardi Black, 8 grams per liter
- Captain Morgan Jamaica Rum, 3 grams per liter
- Havana Club Añejo 7 Años, 4 grams per liter
- Ron Matusalem Solera 7, 3 grams per liter

Honey is a common flavoring agent in rum. Coincidently, dry rum often carries a subtle honey note.

But this statement and others like it are a slap in the face to the likes of Foursquare, whose tradition only knows fermentation, distillation, maturation, and blending. The concept of adding sugar was foreign to Seale, a Barbados native. When he tasted it for the first time, Seale didn't think it was rum. "If they want us to respect them, why don't they declare the product as the rum liqueur it is and not as rum—that is our tradition, how about they respect that!" says Seale, who's quite vocal about his stance on additives.

With all the great rum being produced right now, and with the growing trend of consumers seeking "social justice" and looking to grind their axes on social media, full transparency is the hope of rum's future. Consumers don't seem to mind sugar additives, but they don't care for deception.

There's a growing population of straight whiskey drinkers who demand purity in their spirits. Consumer advocate Wade Woodard, who has reported whiskey brands to the US federal government for label violations (leading to several lawsuits), believes rum needs transparency. Both Woodard and rum consumer activist Steve Leukanech are leading social media assaults against brands using undisclosed sugar.

From Leukanech's perspective, rum is losing potential consumers who prefer whiskey and whose palates are not accustomed to straight shots of sugar. He argues,

> Suppose you order a Bourbon or Scotch neat, and without telling you, the server turns his back and adds some sugar, some vanilla, some Sherry, some Port, some Muscatel, some smoke flavoring, some fruit flavors and maybe a little glycerin. Is it still called a Bourbon or a Scotch? Clearly it isn't; it has become a cocktail, no matter what the server calls it. "Rums" being served up to consumers with undisclosed additives are simply a cocktail in a bottle, marketing them as Rum is fundamentally dishonest and hurts the reputation and value of the true spirit. . . . The use of undisclosed added sugar and other flavorings is perhaps the single most important reason consumers have been reluctant to embrace the concept and pay for premium rums as a class.
>
> Rum products with sugar and other flavorings need to be labeled as such. Without a clear distinction between Pure Rums and Flavored Rum Products the consumer is left bewildered. The unfortunate reality is that many large producers have for so long misled consumers with obfuscation and deceptive statements that they are committed to what has become the status quo.

Unfortunately, rum's labels don't exactly lend themselves to transparency, because few terms are regulated.

CHAPTER 3

RULES & REGULATIONS

WHEN *HARPER'S* MAGAZINE WRITES A RUM STORY, you'd think the rum world would be elated with hopes that the reach of such a magazine could establish new markets. But as is often the case in mainstream coverage, rum was misrepresented by the magazine. "And while no sugar passes through the distillation process into the final spirit, many rums do often deliver more of an apparent 'sweetness' in their flavor profile than other spirits, perhaps with the exception of bourbon," the article stated.

Although rum regulations vary per country, the one thing they all have in common is the use of sugarcane base. Still, some distillers make sorghum or sugar beet spirit and call it rum without government intervention.

A rum fury ensued in blogs and social media. Leading this charge was Matt Pietrek, author of the *Cocktail Wonk* blog, who called the story "misleading . . . to be quite honest, rum is made from fermented sugar, and so is every other distilled spirit," Pietrek wrote, adding that this type of coverage gives the general public the perception that rum is "too sweet."

Other mainstream coverage often focuses on the fact that rum doesn't have a single, uniformly accepted regulation that defines it. Because rum doesn't have widely known uniform standards, the spirit is often seen as something out of the unruly Wild West, and reporters cite the spirit as unregulated. But as Foursquare master distiller Richard Seale points out, this is problematic and disingenuous, as other spirits types are not held to the same overarching global standards.

Whiskey, for example, which is distilled grain, and brandy, which is distilled fruit, do not face the same criticism for not having one central regulator. There are whiskeys made on every continent, and each country has its own rules. It's the same with rum. "If somebody in the Philippines makes fake Filipino whiskey, nobody is saying 'whiskey' is unregulated. But if that happens in rum, people quickly and falsely accuse us of being unregulated," Seale says.

In fact, rum does have many regulations, but the larger problem is that corporate interests overpower rum's predominant region, the Caribbean. This makes it more difficult for the West Indies Rum and Spirits Producers' Association Inc. (WIRSPA) to have the same power as the Scotch Whisky Association (SWA) or the Bureau National Interprofessionnel du Cognac (BNIC)—two organizations that protect Scotch whiskey and Cognac, respectively. In other words, smaller producers such as Hampden and Foursquare cannot compete on a volume basis against the subsidized Captain Morgan in the market. WIRSPA, the organization that represents these smaller producers, has a mere fraction of the government influence wielded by larger publicly traded conglomerates. In other words, the little guy, who's stringent on quality instead of volume, struggles to create regulations that would benefit their products.

Nevertheless, rum regulations exist at all levels of government.

The United Nations says rum shall "be a potable alcoholic distillate obtained exclusively from sugar-cane products; be fermented by the action of yeast or a mixture of yeast and other organisms; or be a mixture of such distillate which has been aged; have the aromatic characteristics specified to rum and may contain caramel, may be flavored with fruit or any other approved botanical substances/flavorings; and contain not less than 37.0 percent of absolute alcohol by volume. . . . Blended rum shall be ethyl alcohol of agricultural origin to which permitted rum flavors have been added."

By this UN standard, rum's sugaring is just fine. But it lacks distillation proofs, still types, and maturation—all of which can be found in other types of spirit. The US regulation adds distillation proof and age requirements:

> Rum is an alcoholic distillate from the fermented juice of sugar cane, sugar cane syrup, sugar cane molasses, or other sugar cane by-products, produced at less than 190° proof in such manner that the distillate possesses the taste, aroma, and characteristics generally attributed to rum, and bottled at not less than 80° proof; and also includes mixtures solely of such distillate . . . If the label of any rum, imported in bottles, contains any statement of age, the rum shall not be released from customs custody for consumption unless accompanied by a certificate issued by a duly authorized official of the appropriate foreign country,

certifying to the age of the youngest rum in the bottle. The age certified shall be the period during which, after distillation and before bottling, the distilled spirits have been stored in oak containers.

Of course, it doesn't help that the US governing body does not strictly enforce these standards. Given its history, you could almost expect the United States to permit distilled shoe leather to be called rum. It has also allowed rums that violate the "youngest rum in the bottle" clause for age-stated rums.

On the other hand, Canada's rum guidelines are quite restrictive. It closely monitors the labels coming into its country. Among its labeling laws for rum, Canada's government notes, "Claims for the age of rum are restricted to the time the rum was stored in small wood. Rum, including any domestic or imported spirit added as flavoring, must be aged in small wood for not less than one year." That means Canadian law mandates "rum" to be aged, a restriction no other powerful country enforces.

On the matter of age, Canada says, "Younger rum can be blended with an older rum, for example 12 year old rum, and under certain conditions retain that age claim. . . The Excise Act permits up to 9.09 percent of the total quantity of absolute ethyl alcohol in the product (which equates to 10 percent by weight) flavoring in the rum." Under Canadian law, rum must be aged a minimum of one year in small wood. Canadians allow for flavoring up to 9.09 percent but only permit age statements in these if the modifier is equal in age to the youngest rum in the batch. In the scenario of a twelve-year-old rum, "if more than 9.09 percent of younger rum is added, the claim 12 year old rum would no longer be acceptable."

Canada also restricts the term *dry*: "In rum . . . where sugar could be added indirectly as part of the flavoring, the range of residual sugar content is very small and not readily detectable. Thus, the use of the term 'dry' could be misleading and should not be used."

While Canada's regulations appear to lead the way in sniffing out deceptive labeling practices, Australia's rum polices have regressed in the past 120 years.

Australia's basic governmental definition lumps rum in with brandy and whiskey, stating that rum must "possess the taste, aroma and other characteristics generally attributed to . . . rum, and must be matured in wood for a minimum period of two years." How is such a statement even found in a government guidebook? What does "characteristics generally attributed to" rum even mean? Does that mean that Captain Morgan spiced rum or the Filipino snake rum are true rum?

Sadly, Australia once had one of the best government definitions on its books, published in 1906: "Australian Standard Rum means rum which complies with the following requisites (a) It must have been distilled wholly from sugar, sugar syrup, molasses, or the refuse of sugar cane, by a pot still or similar process at a strength not exceeding forty-five per cent over proof; (b) It must have been matured, while subject to the control of the Customs, by storage in wood for a period of not less than two years; and (c) It must have been certified by an officer to be pure rum containing all the essential elements of rum."

Of course, the major rum manufacturing nations actually have rum definitions and enforce them. Peru requires rum to be aged in oak for at least one year. Guatemalan rum must be distilled from fermented virgin sugarcane honey, which is molasses prior to crystallization. When molasses is distilled in Guatemala, it is called *aguardiente*. Guatemalan regulations require oak and a barrel-entry proof of no more than 60 percent ABV. Barbados forbids the use of additives.

Venezuelan regulations allow for sugar and flavoring but not the topping of barrels to compensate for evaporation (the angel's share). This is a common practice: the barrel loses spirit, so distillers pour rum from another barrel into the evaporating one. In addition, Venezuelan rum must be aged for a minimum of two years in oak barrels and bottled at no less than 40 percent ABV. Venezuelan distillers are also highly secured, with two gun-carrying soldiers stationed at the facility at all times. There are only two keys to open an aging warehouse—the soldiers have one and the master distiller has the other. When a Venezuelan rum barrel is emptied, it must be reported to the government.

In the rum world, Venezuelan rum makers are often chastised for sugar practices, but they're really quite regulated in comparison to other rum regions.

The bulk of rum's lineage and distilling know-how comes from the Caribbean islands. This Compleat Map of the West Indies *was created in the 1770s.* LIBRARY OF CONGRESS

Each Caribbean island carries its own set of rules. But the Caribbean Community, referred to as CARICOM—an organization of fifteen nations that promote the economic integration and cooperation of the Caribbean—promote the volunteer mark "Authentic Caribbean Rum," indicating that it is under the auspices of the West Indies Rum and Spirits Producers' Association:

- It must be from sugarcane origin.
- It must be fermented and distilled in a CARIFORUM country (one of the fifteeen CARICOM countries or Puerto Rico).
- It must be distilled below 96 percent ABV (95 percent ABV for US product).
- Flavors are not permitted.
- Color must be derived from wood or from caramel (for rounding).
- Must be bottled at 40 percent ABV (37.5 percent ABV where permitted).
- Where a statement of maturity and/or age is given, it shall be that of the youngest distilled spirit in the product.
- The rum shall have been matured in wooden vats.

Currently, Jamaica is near completion of its geographical protection for Jamaican rum, which would require that limestone Jamaican water be used in fermentation; that the rum must be fermented and distilled in Jamaica; and that it contains no additives other than a little caramel coloring, including no sugar or flavors. If there is an age declaration, it must be the age of the minimum barrel in the batch.

Of all the regulations, the island of Martinique has the most stringent. The AOC (Appellation d'Origine Contrôlée) Martinique dictates that its *rhum agricole* rum must be produced from sugarcane grown within twenty-three designated areas. Martinique, an insular region of France, legislates how sugarcane is processed (ground and pressed), and distillation occurs in column stills between 65 percent and 75 percent ABV. Rhum "blanc" Martinique is defined as colorless rum with no more than three months in oak barrels. No rhum with a Martinique designation can be bottled under 40 percent ABV.

While these certainly are not all of the rum regulations, the aforementioned highlight a few of them and certainly put a major hole in the argument that "rum is unregulated." Arguably, the larger problem is what's on the label and the claims companies make regarding rum styles. In a perfect world, the labels would list the production styles to help you predict the flavor potential.

In the meantime, rum thought leaders have created categories that are part geographically influenced and part production oriented. In this context, French-style rums are those made from fresh sugarcane juice, and are often labeled "agricole." English-style rums are made from molasses, generally pot-distilled or at least including a pot-distilled spirit in the blend, and tend to be heavier in flavor. Spanish-style rum is column-distilled and often lighter. All these styles are dictated by the country's original territory owners, such as Spain owning Cuba and Puerto Rico, two islands that make Spanish-style rums. Thus Puerto Rico's Bacardi is a light-bodied rum in the Spanish style.

In his book *Smuggler's Cove: Exotic Cocktails, Rum, and the Cult of Tiki* and at the popular San Francisco bar itself, rum icon Martin Cate splits up the categories by still type and age, with three types of age: lightly aged, one to four years old; aged, five to fourteen years old; and long aged, more than fifteen years old. Cate places Appleton Estate 50 Year in his Pot Still Long Aged category and Dos Maderas 5+3 and 5+5 blends in the blended aged category. If you know Cate's system, you know that Dos Maderas is a blended rum between five and fourteen years old. This could be widely helpful to consumers!

Unfortunately, rum brands only address style on the label when it's a

The French island Martinique is rum's most-regulated region and offers some of the most unique flavor profiles. When you see Martinique AOC, you can trust that the spirit was made to the regulation standards.

Single-barrel *is not a common term or practice in rum. Single barrels are more of a bourbon production technique. However, due to bourbon's single-barrel popularity, a few rum brands have taken advantage of the technique and marketing power.*

regulated term, or when it can influence sales. Some of these terms are not always self-explanatory.

SINGLE BARREL: This is supposed to mean that a single barrel was dumped and bottled, but because this term is not regulated, many rum distillers have abused the term. Richland Rum is one true single barrel you can trust.

SOLERA: A technique used in sherry production, *solera* means stacking barrels on one another and refilling the bottom barrels with the top barrels, thereby mixing together different vintages. But many using *solera* on the label are actually using an adaptation process, in which older lots meet younger barrels in a blending vat and/or wood is added into the process. Only a handful—namely Santa Teresa, Cartavio, and Dictador—employ the true solera system. Cartavio says it takes out 50 percent of the bottom-level rum and refills the barrels with rum from the upper levels.

SINGLE-POT STILL: This means the rum came from only one pot still.

BLENDED: Blended rum is aged pot-still rum and aged column- still rum. In these, the column still *typically* makes up between 50 to 85 percent of the volume, while the pot still adds much of the flavoring backbone.

AGRICOLE: This style of rum comes from fresh sugarcane juice.

LIGHT RUM (ALSO CALLED SILVER OR WHITE): This means the rum has no color. It could have been distilled, cut with water and bottled, or aged and filter-stripped of color. Sugar is sometimes added.

GOLD RUM (ALSO CALLED AMBER): This means it has been aged in wood, with color that offers a golden or amber hue. There are some exceptions, such as Hampden Gold, which is sometimes unaged. Many definitions say this category is stronger in flavor than light rum; this is not always true, as coloring and sugar are often added to the rum.

SPICED RUM: This category has coloring, spices, and flavorings added. However, unlike other categories, spiced rum doesn't hide this fact. It's "spiced" and "sweetened" for all to see. Producers will add cinnamon, caraway, nutmeg, and other spices on top of vanilla and caramel flavors.

DARK RUM: It's often darker in color than gold rum, but this is not always the case.

FLAVORED RUM: Thanks to the popularity of flavored vodka, flavored rum exists to capture the sweet-tooth market. Today, there are dozens of flavored rums, from coconut to orange. By US definition, it's "rum flavored with natural flavoring materials, with or without the addition of sugar, bottled at not less than 30 percent alcohol by volume (60 proof). The name of the predominant flavor shall appear as part of the class and type designation, e.g., 'Butterscotch Favored Rum.'"

OVERPROOF RUM: These rums pack the heat, ranging in proofs from 120 to

160. They're so high in proof that you often can't check them in flight luggage. Unless your palate is made of steel, these aren't recommended for sipping—cocktails only.

PREMIUM RUM, GRAN RESERVA ESPECIAL, XO: Although one could slap "Premium Rum" or "XO" on a bottle of inferior product, these terms typically represent a brand's best attempt at a well-aged rum.

VIEUX: For French Caribbean distillers, vieux means at least three years old.

TRÈS VIEUX: This means even older rums.

HORS D'AGE: Blends of old rums.

NUMBERS: When you see a number on a label, make sure it's accompanied with the word *age* or *años*. If there's no age-signifying word, then it's just a number. Many rum brands will try to place in small print that the number is a rounded number of the rums inside the bottle.

CACHAÇA: This sugarcane spirit enjoys geographical protection in Brazil. It's fermented sugarcane, distilled and bottled between 38 percent and 48 percent ABV at 20 degrees Celsius. Some is unaged, but the aged products are stored in wood, which has no restrictions of origin.

In addition to making incredible rum, Martinique's sailing is thought to be grand, with views of mountains and clear waters. HOUSE OF AGRICOLE

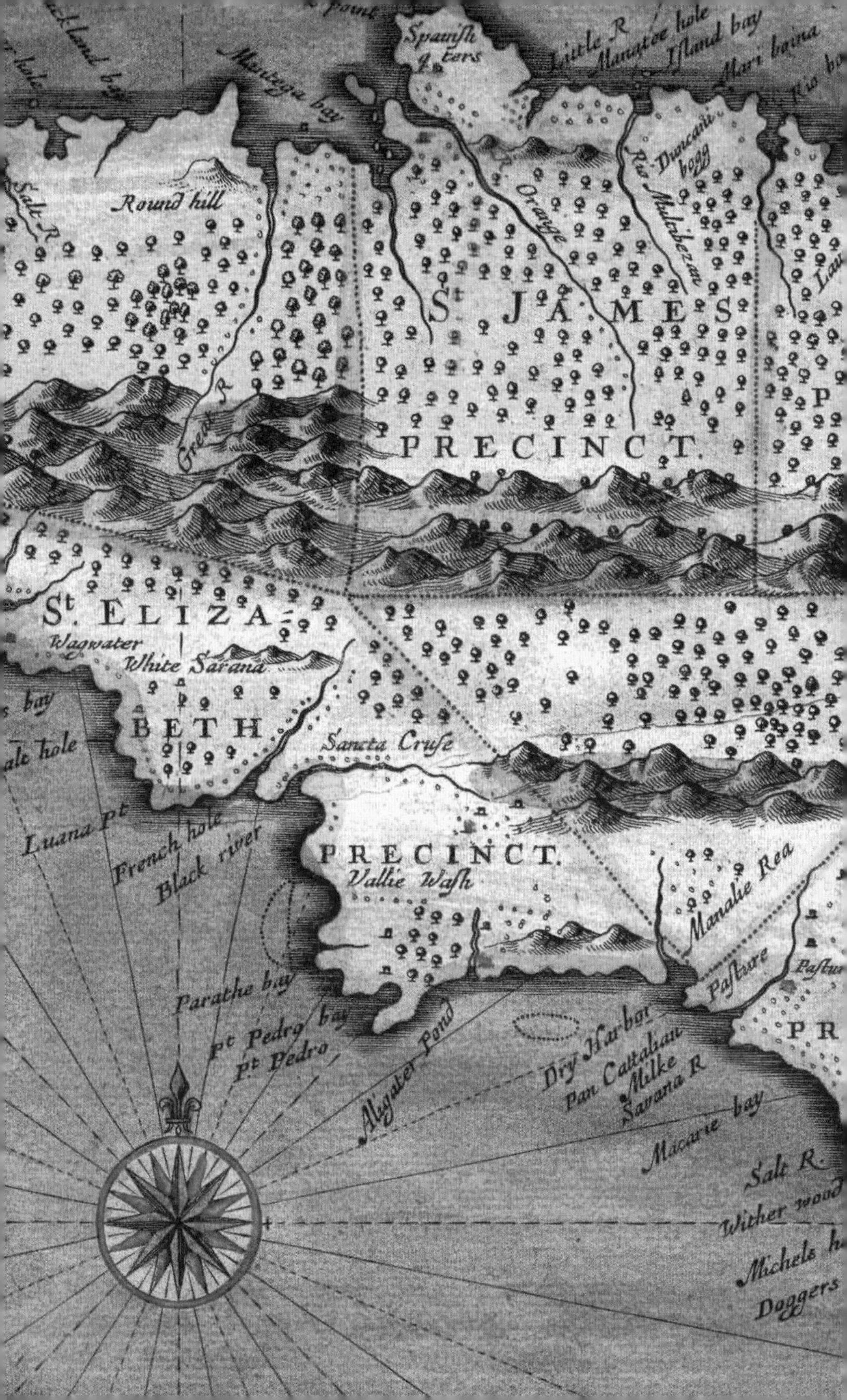

Point

Spanish

Little R.

Manatee hole

Island bay

Mari baina

Rio bo

Musketto bay

Spanish Tiers

Salt R.

Round hill

Orange

Rio Diaварис bogg

Rio Mulebezan

S. JAMES

Liau

P

Land bay

Salt hole

PRECINCT.

St. ELIZA-

Wagwater

White Sarana

BETH

Sancta Cruse

s bay

ale hole

Luana pt

French hole

Black river

PRECINCT.

Vallie Wash

Manatie Rea

Pasture

Pasture

PR

Parathe bay

pt Pedro bay

Pt Pedro

Algvater Pond

Dry Harbor

Pan Cattalian

Milke

Sarana R.

Macarie bay

Salt R.

Wither wood

Michels h

Daggers

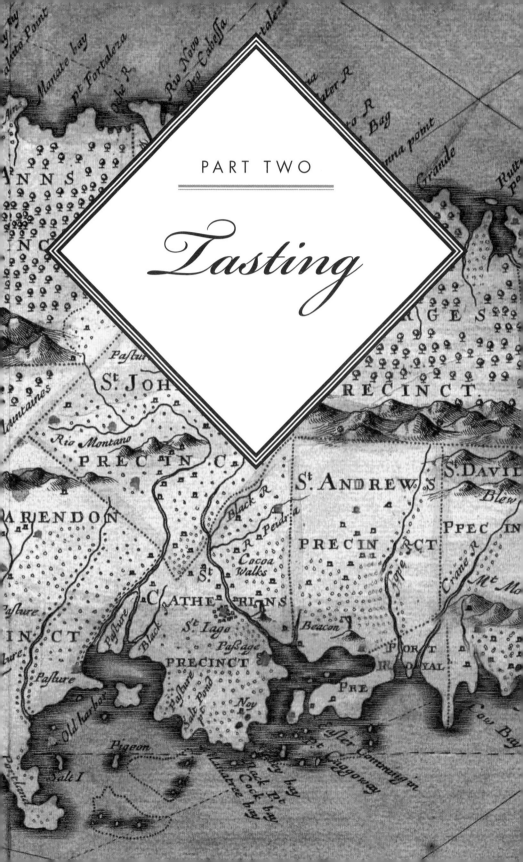

PART TWO

Tasting

TASTING OVERVIEW

WHILE WHISKEY AND BRANDY ATTRACT CONNOISSEURS for their sipping quality, rum is often snubbed due to its reputation as a mixer spirit. However, pound for pound, the world's best rum is every bit as good as the best whiskey or brandy. So, if you're not sipping rum, you should be, and my tasting notes and scores should get you in the right direction.

With that said, traditional whiskey and brandy sippers may need to educate themselves on rum's base—molasses and sugarcane. To truly appreciate rum, you must first understand the raw, appealing nature of molasses. The production chapter gives you a peek into how molasses is made, but you cannot understand the taste without tasting molasses, sugarcane syrup, or sugarcane juice. After all, whiskey drinkers can revert back to breads to understand that spirit's grain base, and brandy drinkers can taste the fruits in their spirit's base.

PRECEDING SPREAD: *Detail of map drawn by John Speed, dated 1676, and printed by Thomas Basset and Richard Chiswell in London, England.* LIBRARY OF CONGRESS
ABOVE: *Tasting rum is a different process than tasting whiskey. Rum typically contains coloring, so the color matters little. The nose is also one of the most amazing experiences in spirits in that you can smell the barrel, sugarcane, and occasionally the sugar. Even a novice palate can pick up the sweetened rums.*

You'll find molasses, cane syrup, and cane juice in many grocery stores. Buy them, smell them, taste them, and you'll come to appreciate the flavor of rum when you taste it—and be disappointed when a rum distiller strips out all of the molasses flavor. Molasses and cane syrup tend to have the texture of processed honey, with a taste that is nothing like sugar. It's pungent, earthy, and slightly sweet.

However, this section is based on my palate, and many reputable tasters may disagree with my opinion. That's why we taste—it's a subjective experience.

In my scores, while I do not penalize brands if they taste like a sugar packet or glass of wine, I'll be less likely to give it a high score than one that is balanced.

What I'm looking for?

First, as with any spirit, I'm looking to validate that it is truly of the category. You can't assess color in rum because so much food coloring is used. But since color doesn't matter to rum's quality anyway, what I'm analyzing is the smell, taste, and finish.

When sampling rum, the nose does not lie. While incredible-smelling bourbons are sometimes flawed on the palate, rum's taste tends to follow the aroma it initially presents. If it smells sweet, it typically tastes sweet. Martinique rum may be the one outlier in this assessment. Their aromas may offer grass or vegetal hints, but not all Martinique rums will pack these notes.

In general, your sense of smell can spot bad rum and save your palate from wasting its time. If rum smells like vodka, I'll immediately question its worth, because vodka has an alcohol-forward nose. Why would I waste my taste buds on alcohol taste? These types of rums are meant for a skilled bartender to mask their flaws. However, if the rum charmingly fills the olfactory area with notes similar to brandy or whiskey, both barrel-aged products, I'll be more interested. In other

Ah, yes, perhaps the most popular drink in the world: the rum and coke. One should never forget the lime. Plantation 3 Stars is a bartender favorite for mixing.

words, I'm first looking for off-putting aromas and their base—sugarcane, an often pungent smell that is delightful to those who enjoy a good cane syrup. Next, I am fascinated when a spirit's base permeates after distillation and barrel aging, which essentially acts as a filter as the spirit ages. From there, I am seeking the flavors, which for rum can range from coconut to saffron.

On the palate, you can really detect the sweet. After the sweet, the spice and nuance set in. You'll find that rum carries the taste of earth, baking ingredients, and some types of baked goods (such as molasses cookies). Rum's mouthfeel is all over the place. Those with additives hit the palate differently, almost quicker, than the rum without additives.

Nonadditive rum feels—not tastes—more like whiskey as it starts on the tip on the tongue and moves back and down the jawline. Meanwhile, the sugared-up rum hits the tongue in the middle like a saltier item and works its way toward the back and forward. Some can still be pleasurable sipping experiences, but they feel different on the palate.

How to Tell Whether Your Rum Has Sugar

Adding sweeteners to rum before bottling is quite common, but brands rarely disclose this fact. If you'd like to find out for yourself, here's how.

- **BUY A HYDROMETER.** This is a basic device used by spirits producers that will scientifically distinguish nondistilled sugars.
- **RUB A BIT OF THE RUM IN YOUR HANDS.** Ideally, you don't do this at a party, where people might question your sanity, but pour a little rum in your hands and rub them together. If your hands feel sticky, you've got sugar.
- **TRUST THE ANTS.** Find an ant pile and pour on a little rum. If they crawl to it, there's definitely some sucrose for their delight.

After your first taste of a rum, the sugared ones will often have a concentration in the middle of your palate, where salts are normally felt.

SCORING

These scoring standards are based on quality within each rum's specific respective category.

59 and below	Not recommended.
60 to 69	Meh. I'd find something else to drink.
70 to 79	Adequate. I'd buy in a pinch.
80 to 89	Good. I'm buying this for my liquor cabinet.
90 to 95	Excellent. I never want to run out of this for as long as I live.
96 to 100	Amazing. A once-in-a-lifetime kind of taste.

CHAPTER 4

UNAGED RUM

IN THIS SECTION, I'M LOOKING FOR FLAVOR. If I detect unwanted properties, such as the taste of shoe polish, I will penalize heavily. I'm also ensuring that the unaged rum is representative of the category—meaning that it doesn't smell or taste like vodka. I will reward base flavor, such as raw sugarcane notes; I find sugarcane coming through to be good distillation technique, and I love this funkiness. I understand that lighter rums do not necessarily have molasses notes, which is fine as long as they are flavorful. Unaged rum is usually mixed, and these scores are based on their mixability and sipping merit.

Unaged or highly filtered rums can be sipped, but their main purpose in life is to be cocktail-consumed.

BALLAST POINT THREE SHEETS CALIFORNIA SMALL BATCH RUM,

40% ABV, CALIFORNIA, UNITED STATES

AROMA: Vanilla and fruit

PALATE: Slightly neutral, but hints of vanilla and nutmeg appear on the finish.

SCORE: 65

HOW TO DRINK: For drinks calling for vodka, this would make an
excellent replacement.

BAYOU SILVER RUM,

40% ABV, LACASSINE, LOUISIANA, UNITED STATES

AROMA: Clean, slight hint of molasses

PALATE: While the aroma doesn't show uniquely rum, the palate does, presenting
molasses, pear, and pineapple. It's very good for an unaged rum.

SCORE: 72

HOW TO DRINK: Mixer only, but solely for cocktails not expecting
rum-forward flavor.

CANE RUN ESTATE ORIGINAL RUM NUMBER 12 BLEND,

40% ABV, CARIBBEAN

AROMA: Somewhat odorless, but hints of fruit appear

PALATE: Void of any sugarcane-base properties, but fruit and a hint of vanilla can
be found.

SCORE: 72

HOW TO DRINK: Use in cocktails calling for vodka.

CHARBONEAU DISTILLERY WHITE RUM, BATCH NO. 10,

40% ABV, MISSISSIPPI, UNITED STATES

AROMA: Ginger, slight hints of hops, grapefruit, and vanilla

PALATE: Extremely unique in taste, layering the palate in powerful citrus notes,
especially grapefruit, followed by molasses cookie, black pepper,
and a bevy of vegetal notes toward the end. The vegetal notes are not
like those of agricole or cachaça. Rather, these skew more toward a
well-crafted moonshine.

SCORE: 80

HOW TO DRINK: This rum just doesn't fit in a traditional rum box, but that's not a
bad thing. Due to the grapefruit notes, it makes an interesting
Hemingway Daiquiri.

CLÉMENT RHUM CANNE BLEUE BLANC AGRICOLE,

50% ABV, MARTINIQUE

AROMA: Raw, earthy, vegetal, grassy, and a bountiful amount of sugarcane

PALATE: Fresh cane juice with pulp, citrus, green apple, oregano, and baking spice.

SCORE: 87

HOW TO DRINK: Use as a whiskey replacement in an Old Fashioned, Brown Derby, Manhattan, and other iconic whiskey drinks.

DON Q CRISTAL,

40% ABV, PUERTO RICO

AROMA: Floral and fruity

PALATE: Alcohol forward and lacks a taste of its molasses base, but there are hints of fruit that are appealing.

SCORE: 70

HOW TO DRINK: Use for mixing only.

(HAMILTON, IMPORTER) DUQUESNE RHUM AGRICOLE,

50% ABV, MARTINIQUE

AROMA: Raw, earthy, vegetal, anise, sugarcane, and palm tree

PALATE: Beautiful, chewy, spicy with hints of black licorice, pepper, vanilla, and caramelized onions.

SCORE: 85

HOW TO DRINK: As part of a cocktail in which you want to taste the sugar-cane-forward base spirit—or for sipping, if you love earth

(HAMILTON, IMPORTER) LA FAVORITE BLANC AOC,

50% ABV, MARTINIQUE

AROMA: Sugarcane, apple, and earth

PALATE: Spicy, with green pepper, sugarcane juice, honey, and pear.

SCORE: 80

HOW TO DRINK: This is a unique sipper but could make some awesome cocktails, especially spice-forward concoctions.

(HAMILTON, IMPORTER) NEISSON BLANC RHUM AGRICOLE,
50% ABV, MARTINIQUE

AROMA: Beach, earth, sugarcane, and peanut

PALATE: Layered, creamy, complex with spice and herbs. This is the perfect unaged spirit, with full expression of its base, sugarcane juice, with citrus nuance, especially grapefruit. Perfect for what it is.

SCORE: 90

HOW TO DRINK: For those who like grappa, this is your new favorite sipper. It's also perfect for cocktails that call for citrus.

(HAMILTON, IMPORTER) NEISSON L'ESPRIT BLANC RHUM AGRICOLE, **70% ABV, MARTINIQUE**

AROMA: Fresh-pressed sugarcane with hints of baked sweet potato, mint, and fresh-cut grass

PALATE: Oh yeah, that's alcohol forward, but rich and layered in sugarcane. It's not quite like sipping sugarcane juice straight from the press, but it's close. Vegetal and vanilla notes too.

SCORE: 89

HOW TO DRINK: Cocktails or sipping if you love high-proof spirits.

ISAUTIER RHUM BLANC AGRICOLE,
55% ABV, RÉUNION

AROMA: This is rhum in its purest form, before a barrel and with its sugarcane essence still intact. Fresh cane juice, molasses, boiling oats, and earth lead the way on this adventurous nose.

PALATE: The higher alcohol is well suited for this flavorful beauty. The chewiness of the mouthfeel gives tastes of granola, dried fruit, hints of oregano, and sautéed mushroom, with just a slight hint of black pepper. This could be sipped neat. But in the hands of the right bartender, this could make amazing cocktails.

SCORE: 99

HOW TO DRINK: Best unaged rum tasted for this book. It's a great sipper if you love spice but will reward your cocktail craving too.

Isautier Rhum Blanc Agricole.

MARGARITAVILLE SILVER RUM, 40% ABV, CARIBBEAN

AROMA: Hints of molasses, rhubarb, and pear

PALATE: First sweetness, then hints of molasses cookie and mint

SCORE: 74

HOW TO DRINK: Rum and Coke

PUERTO ANGEL BLANCO, 40% ABV, OAXACA, MEXICO

AROMA: This is the kind of nose that brings a smile to a rum lover. For an unaged rum, it packs a lot of rich fruit in the form of plantain, baked apple, and bananas Foster, with notes of tilled earth and sugarcane.

PALATE: It's delicate on the palate, with hints of ginger, fruit, and a speckle of spice, but it would also be a great mixing rum.

SCORE: 90

HOW TO DRINK: Great for banana-leaning or other fruit-forward cocktails. Recommended: Banana Daiquiri, in a blender. Add 2 ounces Puerto Angel Blanco, 1 banana, ½ cup coconut milk, ¼ cup caster sugar, 3 cups ice, and blend until smooth.

RHUM BARBANCOURT RHUM WHITE, 43% ABV, HAITI

AROMA: Hints of clove, sugarcane, and pear

PALATE: An astringent taste but clean, with hints of fruit

SCORE: 70

HOW TO DRINK: Use in punch.

RON CARTAVIO SILVER, AGED 2 YEARS AND STRIPPED OF COLOR, 40% ABV, PERU

AROMA: Light in aroma but hints of vanilla and spice

PALATE: This rum has a decent, dry mouthfeel with sweetness and a slight hint of ginger.

SCORE: 80

HOW TO DRINK: Makes an excellent El Presidente.

RON PLATA, 37.5% ABV, SPAIN

AROMA: Light and fruity with a hint of mint

PALATE: Clean, practically tasteless in approach

SCORE: 61

HOW TO DRINK: This makes a good replacement for vodka.

RUM-BAR RUM PREMIUM WHITE OVERPROOF,

63% ABV, JAMAICA

AROMA: Heavy sugarcane, vegetal notes, and grass

PALATE: Pretty rich and rounded, with authentic molasses, cane syrup, and herbs. Spicy finish.

SCORE: 90

HOW TO DRINK: This is a must-have behind the bar. If you're ever in the mood for a boozy daiquiri or mojito, this is your rum. Look for ways to include this overproof rum in your cocktails.

ST. GEORGE UNAGED AGRICOLE RUM,

43%T ABV, CALIFORNIA, UNITED STATES

AROMA: Rawness personified—if you like earth, pine, rich and raw sugarcane juice, and fresh-cut grass, you'll love this nose.

PALATE: There's so much flavor here, but it's not your typical white rum. After the earth, it's vegetal, spice, mint, and a hint of roasted pine nut. This is a love-it-or-hate-it style. I happen to love it and prefer to mix with an unaged rum with tremendous flavor rather than one that presents little nuance.

SCORE: 87

HOW TO DRINK: So unique. This is one that comes without a recommended use, as it's so different. Think funky cocktails, and you've found this rum's home.

SAINT JAMES RHUM BLANC AGRICOLE IMPERIAL BLANC,

40% ABV, MARTINIQUE

AROMA: Vegetal notes, pepper spice, banana, and molasses (Note: This is made from sugarcane juice, not molasses.)

PALATE: Very spicy with nuance of vanilla and nutmeg. The finish is short, with black pepper.

SCORE: 80

HOW TO DRINK: Piña colada

TAILDRAGGER WHITE RUM BATCH 98,

40% ABV, ILLINOIS, UNITED STATES

AROMA: Clean, neutral, with a hint of molasses

PALATE: Very clean and crisp with apple tart, molasses, and a hint of caramel chew

SCORE: 80

HOW TO DRINK: Look for this to replace vodka. But it's not odorless and tasteless. You'll actually taste the rum!

TOPPER'S RHUM CARIBBEAN WHITE,

40% ABV, SINT MAARTEN

AROMA: Slight hints of vanilla and roasted almond

PALATE: Vanilla extract, raspberry, chocolate, and banana

SCORE: 68

HOW TO DRINK: Use in cocktails that require little sugar.

WICKED DOLPHIN SILVER RESERVE,

40% ABV, FLORIDA, UNITED STATES

AROMA: Caramel, toffee, hazelnut, and floral

PALATE: Sweet beginning, with vanilla cake batter and tres leches cake, slowly softening to a subtle caramel. There's a hint of baking spice too.

SCORE: 78

HOW TO DRINK: This makes an interesting Old Fashioned.

OPPOSITE: *In Alameda, California, lies the classic craft distiller St. George Spirits. St. George makes vodka, whiskey, gin, and rum, among other things. Their rums carry a funk that many appreciate.*

WRAY & NEPHEW OVERPROOF RUM WHITE,

63% ABV, JAMAICA

AROMA: Ripe and rich sugarcane with hints of beets, pepper, and a slight hint of vanilla

PALATE: When assessing such a high-proof spirit, you must be prepared for the bite. But it really doesn't come here. The spirit is smoother than some 40 percent ABV spirits, offering up vegetal, molasses, and spice notes. Although the alcohol is felt toward the end, it does not overtake such a beautiful raw expression.

SCORE: 90

HOW TO DRINK: If you're looking for boozy cocktails, this warrants consideration. It's especially great mixed with vermouth. Can you say overproof rum Manhattan?

Rum is an amazing mixer. Wray & Nephew Overproof Rum White is an extremely flexible high-proofed spirit for cocktails.

CHAPTER 5

AGED RUM

IN THIS CHAPTER, YOU'LL FIND THE BEAUTIFUL RUMS FROM AROUND THE WORLD THAT HAVE BEEN AGED IN BARRELS. Here, I'm looking for flavor not derived from additives. If a brand tastes like a sugar packet, it will be penalized. If it's sweet but nuanced, that's more acceptable than artificial sweetness. I look for complexity, mouthfeel, and finish.

Unlike in Chapter 4, my scores here are based more on sipping merit and not mixability, but I certainly appreciate the use of of an aged rum in cocktails. For those reaching scores 90 and above, I've offered a special cigar recommendation. It's a treat!

Aged rum offers some of the world's best sipping moments. When paired with a cigar, great rum offers pure bliss.

ADMIRAL RODNEY EXTRA OLD, 40% ABV, SAINT LUCIA

AROMA: Vanilla, baked apples, macaroons, marzipan, baked pear, fried peaches, citrus, cinnamon, and molasses cookie dough

PALATE: Balanced, complex, marriage of fruit, spice, coconut, hazelnut, and toasted almond. It's soft and mouth-coating, with a strong coconut-forward finish.

SCORE: 92

HOW TO DRINK: This is for sipping only. If you want to make cocktails with this gorgeous rum, you may be subject to imprisonment in Saint Lucia.

CIGAR PAIRING: Cubita. A coconut note brings out the coconut in the rum.

APPLETON ESTATE 12-YEAR-OLD, 43% ABV, JAMAICA

AROMA: Beautiful floral over fruit and oak, with hints of apricots and pineapple and a slight hint of molasses

PALATE: It comes quick with spice but slowly softens for vanilla, pome, caramel, and orange marmalade, with a slight hint of smoke. It's perfectly balanced and never shows one note more prominently than the other. A long finish gives a hint of baked apple.

SCORE: 90

HOW TO DRINK: You'll certainly taste the age if used in a cocktail. Too much ice could dilute this rum.

CIGAR PAIRING: Look for a thick cigar, such as a Rocky Patel 1992.

APPLETON ESTATE 21-YEAR-OLD, 43% ABV, JAMAICA

AROMA: Every now and then, a rum comes along and captures your heart and soul. This is the perfect nose, with beautiful roasted nuts, cocoa, toasted oak, campfire smoke, spice, rich vanilla, orange peel, soured cherry mash, and plum pudding.

PALATE: The palate follows what the aroma offered, showcasing long and complex dried apricot, baked apple, cinnamon, nutmeg, allspice, ginger, baked rye bread, and hints of demerara sugar and black pepper. It's balanced and complex with a coating mouthfeel lining every inch of the palate. This flawless rum finishes for a solid two minutes, tingling with a warm touch of cinnamon.

SCORE: 94

HOW TO DRINK: Under no circumstances should this be used in a cocktail. This sipping rum is a little slice of Jamaican heaven.

CIGAR PAIRING: Ramón Allones Habana. The rum's ginger and spice bring out the coffee and earth in the cigar.

Aged rum offers some of the world's best sipping moments. When paired with a cigar, great rum offers pure bliss. Appleton 21-Year-Old is one of the world's best rums and is widely available in the United States.

When assessing cigars, look for a tight roll, and the fewer the stems the better. To determine if it's too dry, apply slight pressure and rotate it near your ear. If you hear a crinkle, it's too dry.

APPLETON ESTATE RESERVE BLEND,

40% ABV, JAMAICA

AROMA: Rich notes of baked apple pie, molasses cookies, caramel, oak, daisies, and a hint of vanilla

PALATE: Chocolate, apple turnover, raw green apple, pumpkin pie, slight hint of pepper, and baked sugar cookie. Finishes medium with a Red Delicious apple.

SCORE: 86

HOW TO DRINK: Mai tai

APPLETON ESTATE SIGNATURE BLEND,

40% ABV, JAMAICA

AROMA: Fruit forward with hints of vanilla, caramel, and a hint of tobacco, followed by oak and molasses

PALATE: True balance. No one note overtaking the other. Velvety on the mouth-feel, with gingerbread and no-bake cookies standing out over spice, fruit, and nutmeg. Finishes short with a taste of apple.

SCORE: 87

HOW TO DRINK: This is a solid sipper, but you'll find this blend really pops in rum drinks that reward flavor.

BACARDI 8-YEAR-OLD,

40% ABV, PUERTO RICO

AROMA: Vanilla, oak, eucalyptus, and hint of roasted almond

PALATE: Cola, caramel syrup, nutmeg, roasted cashew, and pine nut. Medium finish.

SCORE: 83

HOW TO DRINK: This is an excellent mixer and holds its own as a sipper.

BAD BITCH RUM SPANISH MARIE,

40% ABV, KEY WEST, FLORIDA, UNITED STATES

AROMA: Chocolate, baking spices, orange, and coffee

PALATE: Baking spices and citrus hit, followed by bittersweet chocolate, but an alcohol taste cuts the flavors short. The spices and citrus offer some pleasant taste though.

SCORE: 70

HOW TO DRINK: Old Fashioned

BALCONES TEXAS RUM,

63% ABV, TEXAS, UNITED STATES

AROMA: The red color makes one think the aroma could be intense—and that it is, with barrel char, anise, coffee, and whiffs of vanilla, mulch, and fresh-cut oak.

PALATE: There's a chocolate bitterness that turns to wood, and an anise that is pleasant. But the wood-forward notes mask the molasses undertones. There's potential here that opens up with water.

SCORE: 70

HOW TO DRINK: Use in drinks calling for overproofed rum.

BARRELL BATCH 01,

137.74 PROOF, JAMAICA

AROMA: Beautiful fruit, molasses, apple, pear, and strawberry, then brown sugar, caramel, cinnamon, and apricot

PALATE: Spice, plum pudding, orange peel, marzipan, pecan, chocolate, and honey over hints of pepper, green apple, and coconut. Finishes long and fruity.

SCORE: 90

HOW TO DRINK: Sipping only. Bourbon drinkers will love the rum's body and uniqueness in flavor.

CIGAR PAIRING: Oliva Serie V Torpedo. The nuttiness grabs a hold of the marzipan and pecan notes in the rum, and a beautiful pairing abounds.

BAYOU SELECT RUM,

40% ABV, LACASSINE, LOUISIANA, UNITED STATES

AROMA: Botanicals, herbs, coffee, spice, wood chips, and varnish

PALATE: Balanced approach of caramel, vanilla, spice, and an undertone of sweet

SCORE: 79

HOW TO DRINK: Use for cocktails only. This will work well in unsugared drinks.

CHARBAY 2005 DOUBLE AGED RUM,

68.5% ABV, CALIFORNIA, UNITED STATES

AROMA: Think vanilla cake batter, marshmallow, fresh-baked molasses cookies, nutmeg, coffee, hazelnut, maple, and a hint of baked oats

PALATE: Whoa. This has the proof and the flavor, with marzipan, fried dough, chocolate, granola, cinnamon roll, roasted carrot, and burnt Rice Krispies Treats. Quite delicious, with a long finish and a hint of fruit.

SCORE: 90

HOW TO DRINK: Sip only.

CIGAR PAIRING: Graycliff Chateau Grand Cru President offers a hint of granola, burns medium, and brings out the cinnamon in the rum.

CHARBONEAU GOLD RUM,
40% ABV, NATCHEZ, MISSISSIPPI, UNITED STATES

AROMA: Sawdust, hints of clove, cola, cinnamon, hint of nutmeg

PALATE: Apple, cinnamon, pumpkin, and slight hint of molasses cookie

SCORE: 78

HOW TO DRINK: This rum is worthy cocktail mixer.

CLÉMENT RHUM VIEUX AGRICOLE VSOP,
40% ABV, MARTINIQUE

AROMA: Dried apricot, roasted almond, roasted walnut, rich caramel, baked apple, and nutmeg

PALATE: Very similar mouthfeel to a Lowlands Scotch. It's light and fruity, with notes of honey, dried apricot, pear, grapefruit, and a slight hint of tobacco. Medium finish.

SCORE: 87

HOW TO DRINK: This really needs to be sipped neat. It also makes a lovely rum sidecar: 2 ounces Clément VSOP, ¾ ounce lemon juice, and 1 ounce Grand Marnier.

COCKSPUR FINE RUM,
40% ABV, BARBADOS

AROMA: Oak, chocolate, anise, orange, and a slight hint of molasses

PALATE: Very light and neutral, with hints of citrus and chocolate

SCORE: 77

HOW TO DRINK: This doesn't fall in the same line as most Barbados rums and is more similar to Puerto Rican styles: lighter in body and meant for easy cocktail mixing.

The Barbados-based West Indies Distillery serves as a contract distiller. It produces Malibu and country music star Kenny Chesney's Blue Chair rum, among others.

COCKSPUR GOLD RUM, 40% ABV, BARBADOS

AROMA: Slightly neutral, with oak undertones and slight hints of coconut, molasses, and caramel

PALATE: Salted caramel, molasses cookie, oak, roasted pecan, raw walnut, dried walnut, and dried apricot. Even with these beautiful notes, an alcohol forwardness takes hold and hurts its finish.

SCORE: 80

HOW TO DRINK: Use in a daiquiri.

COCKSPUR VSOR 12, 40% ABV, BARBADOS

AROMA: Rich caramel, baking spice, molasses, almond butter, and a hint of ocean air

PALATE: Spicy, dark chocolate, vanilla wafer, and butterscotch. Long finish with a hint of caramel.

SCORE: 86

HOW TO DRINK: This is a decent sipper, but the complexity just isn't there to make it a must-have sipper. It also makes good cocktails.

CRUZAN ESTATE DIAMOND, LIGHT RUM 5 YEARS,
40% ABV, SAINT CROIX
AROMA: Reminiscent of vodka, with touches of oak, mint, and a hint of caramel

PALATE: For 40 percent ABV, it's incredibly hot, with slight hints of vanilla extract. But it's a neutral flavor. Its saving grace is that it makes a decent daiquiri, but it's not a sipping rum.

SCORE: 70

HOW TO DRINK: Use in a daiquiri.

DAMOISEAU XO, 42% ABV, GUADELOUPE
AROMA: Lemon zest, orange peel, blood orange, dandelion, fresh-cut grass, and vanilla

PALATE: Citrus, pickled melon, hard lemon candies, cinnamon, vanilla cake batter, and a hint of white pepper

SCORE: 85

HOW TO DRINK: Sip neat or use in cocktails that call for citrus.

DAMOISEAU XO RHUM VIEUX, 42% ABV, GUADELOUPE
AROMA: Think cinnamon. It's in the front, middle, and end, with an in-between of crushed raspberries, molasses, pumpkin, red pepper, and allspice.

PALATE: Gorgeous, complex, accentuating the nose. From cinnamon to Red Hots, it's ripe with the lovely baking spice and with hints of berries, oak, pepper, and vanilla. Long, beautiful finish with a hint of citrus rind.

SCORE: 89

HOW TO DRINK: Sip neat.

DIPLOMÁTICO AMBASSADOR, 47% ABV, VENEZUELA
FINISHED IN PEDRO XIMÉNEZ BARRELS
AROMA: Cherry, black currant, vanilla, caramel, marzipan, and chocolate

PALATE: My first thought is that this is a mouthful of cherries, almonds, and chocolate. A trace amount of molasses cookies appears over baking spices, spearmint, and a slight hint of black licorice. Pronounced vanilla appears for a long finish.

SCORE: 88

HOW TO DRINK: Rum punch

DIPLOMÁTICO RESERVA EXCLUSIVA,

40% ABV, VENEZUELA

AROMA: Crushed almonds, vanilla, and caramel

PALATE: Extraordinarily sweet, with a sweet aftertaste. All I taste is sugar, which is not the case in other expressions from this brand.

SCORE: 74

HOW TO DRINK: Cocktails that do not require sugar. The amount of sweetness in this rum will carry over for a sweetness factor.

DIPLOMÁTICO SINGLE VINTAGE 2000,

43% ABV, VENEZUELA

AROMA: Toffee, burnt sugar, caramel, vanilla, oak, and fresh-baked wheat bread

PALATE: The minute it hits the tongue, the sugar is detected. But thankfully, it's not oversaturated. A plethora of nuttiness and rich vanilla comes through, knocking back the sugar. Candy apple, brown sugar, and cinnamon Jolly Rancher come through toward the end. Amazingly, this rum starts slow but finishes strong and long for a good two minutes, with a lovely touch of cinnamon.

SCORE: 92

HOW TO DRINK: Sip.

CIGAR PAIRING: Rocky Patel Cigar Fifteenth Anniversary has a richness that cuts the sweetness and bolsters the cinnamon.

DEADHEAD RUM,

40% ABV, MEXICO

AROMA: Oak, coffee, fruit, floral, almond extract, and mulch

PALATE: Think coffee and latte, then vanilla, toffee, and hazelnut with a touch of whipped cream. Short finish disappoints but offers a subtle pumpkin spice.

SCORE: 82

HOW TO DRINK: This makes a great replacement in cocktails calling for Irish whiskey.

DON PANCHO ORIGENES 8-YEAR-OLD, 40% ABV, PANAMA

AROMA: Vanilla, butterscotch, hint of anise

PALATE: Sugar-packet oversweet but slight nuance with various fruits

SCORE: 78

HOW TO DRINK: If you'd like a lighter Old Fashioned, this is the perfect rum.

DON PANCHO ORIGENES 18-YEAR-OLD, 40% ABV, PANAMA

AROMA: Blackberry, black currant, raspberry jam, strawberry—really, it offers a strikingly similar nose to port. There's so much fruit here it almost makes me question whether it's rum.

PALATE: Despite the aroma, this beautiful and complex taste says it's most certainly rum, with vanilla, whipped cream, coconut, orange peel, chocolate, and just a hint of cinnamon, with a long and luscious toffee-forward finish.

SCORE: 92

HOW TO DRINK: Sip.

CIGAR PAIRING: Avo Domaine. A butteriness in this cigar complements the creaminess of the rum.

Don Pancho Origenes 18-Year-Old.

DON PANCHO ORIGENES 30-YEAR-OLD, 40% ABV, PANAMA

AROMA: Chocolate pie from the oven, baked vanilla muffin, cherry blossom, rose petal, oak, apricot, and a hint of banana

PALATE: Pure poetry on the tongue. Think burnt pie crust, with its edges crisp and a soft vanilla custard in the middle, while an explosion of roasted almond, dried apricot, and warm baked peaches follow. Hints of tobacco and marzipan accompany an assortment of chocolates from dark to milk. Finally, it finishes long with hints of hazelnut, cinnamon, and vanilla. It's rare to find a spirit in such perfect harmony.

SCORE: 93

HOW TO DRINK: Sip.

CIGAR PAIRING: Joya de Nicaragua Cuatro Cinco Reserva Especial's spiciness somehow cuts the sweetness and strengthens the almonds and apricot of the rum.

DON Q AÑEJO, 40% ABV, PUERTO RICO

AROMA: Vanilla extract, caramel, vanilla, banana, sugar cookie, gingerbread, and spice

PALATE: Some rums come across as so balanced it almost hurts the spirit, because no one note truly stands out. This is the case here. It's warm, balanced, cinnamon, pear, and allspice. Nuanced.

SCORE: 89

HOW TO DRINK: Sip.

DON Q GRAN AÑEJO, 40% ABV, PUERTO RICO

AROMA: Vanilla bean, coriander, cherry, cola, allspice, dried apricot, coffee, and a hint of nutmeg

PALATE: Crème brûlée, vanilla custard, and bittersweet chocolate over peach, roasted pecan, earth, and a slightly astringent mouthfeel. Medium vanilla finish.

SCORE: 89

HOW TO DRINK: Lovely to sip, or use in cocktails that call for aged rum.

DOORLY'S 8-YEAR-OLD, 40% ABV, BARBADOS

AROMA: Beautiful up-front notes of caramel, baked apple pie fresh out of the oven, and cinnamon; with hints of canned peaches and pear

PALATE: Velvety mouthfeel down to the jawline with an overwhelming rice pudding note with spice, grape, and caramel. Although these notes seem few, they're very pronounced and delicious, making for a long and balanced finish.

SCORE: 90

HOW TO DRINK: Sip.

CIGAR PAIRING: Romeo by Romeo y Julieta Piramide. This really high-strength cigar packs some black pepper that brings out more spice in Doorly's.

DOORLY'S 12-YEAR-OLD, 40% ABV, BARBADOS

AROMA: It's almost like standing in the middle of a French bakery, surrounded by savory and sweet, with caramel, vanilla, cotton candy, hints of red chili cooking, and a little earth.

PALATE: Vibrant and rounded banana, pineapple, coconut, and green chili. This has all the makings of a great sipping rum, especially when the spice and coconut note meet rich caramel at the end. Fine work by the barrel here, as it finishes long and strong.

SCORE: 92

HOW TO DRINK: Sip.

CIGAR PAIRING: Brick House Toro, a gorgeous mild cigar with hints of fruit and leather that complement the rum's fruit and bring out some leather not in the rum alone.

EL DORADO 12-YEAR-OLD, 40% ABV, GUYANA

AROMA: Molasses, petrol, vanilla, baked stone fruit, prune, and brown sugar

PALATE: Vanilla forward followed by burnt butter, brown sugar, hazelnut, and coffee. Residual syrup hangs around for a medium finish.

SCORE: 84

HOW TO DRINK: This is a sweet rum but could play nice as a sipper for dessert. Look for citrus-forward cocktails to mix with it.

FLOR DE CAÑA 12, 40% ABV, NICARAGUA

AROMA: Vanilla, sugar, burnt toast, and a hint of molasses

PALATE: Extremely soft but bursting with coconut, caramel, and a hint of cola

SCORE: 80

HOW TO DRINK: Daiquiri

FLOR DE CAÑA 18, 40% ABV, NICARAGUA

AROMA: Coffee, leather, nuts, caramel, cigar box, and oak

PALATE: Bitterness over vanilla, chocolate, coconut, and cream. It's not very sweet, but it's expressive, with dates and other dried fruit. Then, toward the end, cola, toffee, and hazelnut with a bittersweet chocolate finish.

SCORE: 90

HOW TO DRINK: Neat

CIGAR PAIRING: Montecristo White Belicoso. The lightness of the cigar matches the softness of the rum.

FLOR DE CAÑA 25 "SLOW AGED," 40% ABV, NICARAGUA

AROMA: Vibrant with vanilla, brown sugar, and hints of banana and black pepper

PALATE: There's an interesting rice pudding note over pronounced vanilla and lemon tart. But an unwanted astringent-forward taste enters the picture and quashes the appeal. Still, on second taste, while still astringent, the warm and powerful vanilla really comes through.

SCORE: 84

HOW TO DRINK: Use in cocktails.

FLOR DE CAÑA GRAN RESERVA 7-YEAR-OLD, 40% ABV, NICARAGUA

AROMA: Light vanilla, oak, and earth

PALATE: Velvety on the palate, caramel, cinnamon, chocolate milk, and a hint of nutmeg. Finishes medium.

SCORE: 82

HOW TO DRINK: This is a light sipper that has the meat to be a standout as a rum-dominant addition to cocktails. It makes for great daiquiris, mai tais, and pretty much any lighter rum cocktail.

FOURSQUARE 2006 SINGLE BLENDED RUM,

DOUBLE MATURATION, 3 YEARS EX-BOURBON BARRELS AND
7 YEARS EX-COGNAC, 62% ABV, BARBADOS

AROMA: One of the most amazing rum noses you'll ever come across. Complex and spine tingling. Nuanced caramel, rich banana, vanilla, pineapple, passion fruit, dried apricot, dried orange peel, cigar box, rose petal, dark cherry, roasted nuts, and a hint of smoke.

PALATE: So velvety and creamy. Hard to believe it's barrel strength, but the oily notes just jump right out, leading with butterscotch, custard, crème brûlée, dates, raisins, roasted almonds, pecan pie, tobacco, dried apricot, black

Led by distiller Richard Seale, Foursquare Distillery is rapidly becoming one of the world's premier rum distiller. The distillery sits on a historic sugarcane plantation that dates back to the 1600s.

pepper, and slight hints of molasses, orange peel, and mustard seed. This finishes extremely long, up to four minutes, with a hint of cinnamon. It's flawless in every way.

SCORE: 100

HOW TO DRINK: Sip neat. Don't you dare add ice. Don't you dare mix it in a cocktail. Give this beautiful rum the respect it deserves and drink it at full strength.

CIGAR PAIRING: Davidoff Millennium Blend Series Robusto. A buttery mouth-feel coats the palate and allows this beautiful high-proof spirit to cut the fat. It's sublime.

FOURSQUARE 2013 HABITATION VELIER SINGLE-POT RUM,

64% ABV, BARBADOS

AROMA: Molasses, sugar cookie, oak, cherrywood, and tobacco

PALATE: Very rich and layered. Chocolate, buttered sweet potato, dark fruit, caramel, vanilla, brown sugar, and baked apples. Finishes medium, but a heavy spice prominently appears.

SCORE: 90

HOW TO DRINK: Not recommended for cocktails because it deserves to be sipped on its own. Perhaps add two pieces of ice or a splash of water if you're queasy about the proof.

CIGAR PAIRING: Cohiba Esplendido has beautiful fruit that becomes extremely vibrant after a sip of this single-pot-still rum.

Founded by Italian raconteur Luca Gargano, Habitation Velier, the House of Pure Single Rums, selects rums from distilleries and bottles them. They are not available in the United States.

FOURSQUARE PORT CASK FINISH 9-YEAR-OLD,

BOURBON AND PORT WOOD, 40% ABV, BARBADOS

AROMA: Think Spanish desserts: custards, nuts, peaches, marzipan, and coconut. Hints of chocolate and citrus.

PALATE: Beautiful mouthfeel, drenching the palate in marzipan, fried coconut and almond bread, pumpkin, nutmeg, caramel, nuanced vanilla, and raw almonds. Slight hints of baked apples and cinnamon.

SCORE: 91

HOW TO DRINK: Sip neat. Or make a unique cocktail: 2 ounces Foursquare Port Cask, 1 ounce port, ¼ ounce fresh lemon juice. Stir and serve over ice.

CIGAR PAIRING: J. Fuego 777 is a mild cigar with a creaminess that complements the lighter, but pronounced, rum.

FLYING DUTCHMAN DARK RUM, NO. 3,

AGED FOR A MINIMUM OF 3 YEARS, 40% ABV, NETHERLANDS

AROMA: With an explosion of sweet from caramel and slow-baking sugar cookies permeating from the oven, it's complex with its sweeter approach, offering up hints of fruit and spice.

PALATE: Layered, rich; complex with notes of almonds, roasted walnuts, pear, peach, dried apricot, banana, and hint of tobacco. It finishes strong and long, with a beautiful pecan pie note.

SCORE: 90

HOW TO DRINK: Sip neat.

CIGAR PAIRING: Arturo Fuente 8-5-8 packs a hint of banana that becomes nuanced with a sip of this rum.

FLYING DUTCHMAN NO. 1,

AGED FOR A MINIMUM OF 1 YEAR,
40% ABV, NETHERLANDS

AROMA: Wood, coffee, peanut butter, leather, earth, and vanilla

PALATE: Rich and rounded, with notes of nuts, honey, marzipan, smoke, corn shell, chocolate, and tobacco

SCORE: 88

HOW TO DRINK: Sip.

FLYING DUTCHMAN PX DISTILLED 2012,

40% ABV, NETHERLANDS

AROMA: An in-your-face sherry nose with a mesh of walnuts and apricot, masking the slight hints of honey and pipe tobacco

PALATE: Here, too, we find the sherry dominance, but the palate also offers a burnt graham cracker, molasses, and honeycomb. The medium finish presents spice. If you love sherry, this is up your alley.

SCORE: 84

HOW TO DRINK: Sip.

Most rum distillers age in used bourbon barrels. On occasion, a distiller will age in used port, sherry, cognac, and other types of barrels to bring out additional flavor from the respective woods.

GOSLING'S BLACK SEAL 80 PROOF BLACK RUM,
40% ABV, BERMUDA

AROMA: Berries, vanilla extract, cherry pie, cola, and a hint of mint

PALATE: This distinct flavor coats the palate with cherry cola, blueberries, brown sugar, buttered pancakes with maple syrup, and a hint of spearmint. Coffee comes in toward the end for a medium finish.

SCORE: 80

HOW TO DRINK: Dark 'N Stormy

GOSLING'S FAMILY RESERVE RUM, **40% ABV, BERMUDA**

AROMA: Mouthwatering notes of cocoa, cola, coconut, caramel, dark chocolate melting in a saucepan, burnt sugar, dried fruits, chamomile tea, and cherrywood. There's definitely a lot going on here.

PALATE: The fruit endures, offering citrus, peach, pear, dried apricot, and dark cherries, followed by cola and hints of rhubarb, dark chocolate, pumpkin, and caramel. On a long finish, there's a touch of walnut-shell bitterness that's memorable.

SCORE: 88

HOW TO DRINK: Dark 'N Stormy

GOSLING'S GOLD SEAL, **40% ABV, BERMUDA**

AROMA: Floral, citrus, oak, and caramel

PALATE: Nice wood, vanilla, molasses, and a hint of coconut

SCORE: 80

HOW TO DRINK: This is a great mixing rum.

The name Dark 'N Stormy is a trademark of Gosling's.
SHUTTERSTOCK

HAMILTON 86, DEMERARA RIVER, 43% ABV, GUYANA

AROMA: Beauty captivates the nose, with baked apple pie, cinnamon, cane syrup, maple, caramel, vanilla, oak, and a hint of the sea

PALATE: Balance: no one note over takes the other, with notes all coming at the same time. The sweetness and bitterness of chocolate and the richness of caramel meet the sublime dried and baked fruits, with subtle baking spices appearing in a long and lasting finish.

SCORE: 93

HOW TO DRINK: Sip.

CIGAR PAIRING: ACID Blondie. The sweetness of both bring out a lovely pairing.

HAMILTON 151 MINISTRY OF RUM COLLECTION OVERPROOF, 75.5% ABV, GUYANA

AROMA: Molasses, vanilla, and fruit

PALATE: Heavy molasses, tobacco leaf, oak, and cocoa

SCORE: 80

HOW TO DRINK: Well, it's a masculine, heavy, very high-proof rum. So look for cocktails that call for overproof rums, but be sure you want these flavors, because it will dominate whatever it's mixed with.

(HAMILTON, IMPORTER) COEUR RHUM, LA FAVORITE AMBRE AOC MARTINIQUE, 50% ABV, MARTINIQUE

ABOUT: 3 to 8 years old in used bourbon barrels

AROMA: Caramel, vanilla, oak, mint, and hints of chocolate

PALATE: Sliced apple meets spice, with under- and overtones of canned red and black fruits. The lingering spice just sits there, finally developing into a pepper that complements the hints of vanilla, baked fruit, and caramel to come. Finishes long with spice.

SCORE: 91

HOW TO DRINK: Sip neat.

CIGAR PAIRING: Arturo Fuente. The fruit in both make for a great pairing.

HAMILTON DUQUESNE ESB,

40% ABV, MARTINIQUE

AROMA: Lots going on. French bakery meets an American pastry chef. The nuance in baked goods is prominent. Breads, muffins, vanilla batter, chocolate wafers, cinnamon rolls. It's all here.

PALATE: Unlike the nose, the taste skews toward oak, tobacco, and spice. It's a very interesting study of how a nose doesn't match the palate. Nonetheless, it's tasty enough to reward a spot in your liquor cabinet.

SCORE: 85

HOW TO DRINK: Use in cocktails.

HAMILTON JAMAICAN POT STILL BLACK RUM,

46.5% ABV, JAMAICA

AROMA: Medicinal, coffee grounds, caramel, oak, and mulch

PALATE: The notes are few, but they are extraordinary on the palate: raw cane juice, apple, citrus, chocolate, hints of anise, caramel, and earth. This is very reminiscent of pre-Prohibition Jamaican rum—not many notes, but every one is extremely pronounced.

SCORE: 89

HOW TO DRINK: Sip.

HAMILTON JAMAICAN POT STILL GOLD,

46.5% ABV, JAMAICA

AROMA: Cane juice, sea air, oak, and floral

PALATE: The palate comes in with an assortment of cane-related notes, from molasses and cane syrup to juice and a speck of burnt sugar. Then oatmeal, coffee, milk stout, and burnt cornbread. Finishes short, with a hint of apple.

SCORE: 82

HOW TO DRINK: Use in cocktails.

(HAMILTON, IMPORTER) LA FAVORITE AMBRE AOC MARTINIQUE RHUM, 72% ABV, MARTINIQUE

AROMA: Raw and rich with pronounced cane juice, molasses (even though none is used), ground peanuts, canola oil, and oak

PALATE: Uniqueness comes to mind when an explosion of pepper hits, followed by butter-fried sushi rice, earthiness, cane juice, and hints of tart and sweetness. Finishes sharp with a hint of red pepper. This may be the best mixing rum from Martinique. Its unique flavor profile makes it so desirable for a master mixologist.

SCORE: 88

HOW TO DRINK: Sip or entrust with a great bartender.

(HAMILTON, IMPORTER) NEISSON 15-YEAR-OLD FRENCH OAK, 44.7% ABV, MARTINIQUE

AROMA: If heaven had a smell, I imagine this is it for a lover of aged spirits. Coated with butterscotch, toffee, caramel, vanilla, complex oak, hints of saddle leather, an array of baking chocolate, nutmeg, cinnamon, scores of baked fruit, and slight hints of ginger, cumin, and allspice. In my career, I've nosed many amazing spirits, and the truly exceptional all have this "it" quality that makes your neck hairs stand up. This nose has the "it."

PALATE: Heaven continues with complexity covering the palate with cinnamon, gingerbread cookie, caramel, vanilla, raw coconut, coconut in German chocolate cake, dark chocolate, milk chocolate, marshmallow, and tobacco, with slight hints of barbecue smoke, pepper, almond butter, and saltwater taffy. This is truly exceptional.

SCORE: 99

HOW TO DRINK: Sip only. Should you mix in a cocktail, the rum gods will punish you.

CIGAR PAIRING: Angelenos Toro. A gingerbread explosion occurs when the palate meets this smoke and this rum.

(HAMILTON, IMPORTER) NEISSON RHUM ESB, 50% ABV, MARTINIQUE

AROMA: Now, this is interesting. There's a bevy of oak, from freshly cut to toasted and charred to a slight hint of a smoldering campfire. This is followed by medicinal and hints of caramel, baked bread, and anise.

PALATE: It's bright, clean, and delivering fruit—especially apple—with hints of sweet and jalapeño over a touch of green pepper.

SCORE: 82

HOW TO DRINK: Use in cocktails.

(HAMILTON, IMPORTER) NEISSON RÉSERVE SPÉCIALE, 42% ABV, MARTINIQUE

AROMA: Think walking into a coffee shop known for its pastries. There's an assortment of coffee, pastries, and vanilla lingering with roasted nuts and tobacco.

PALATE: This was made for a bourbon drinker looking to enter rum. It packs the heat you want with layers of flavor—notably pancake, coffee, vanilla, caramel, spice, and a mouthfeel that dances between mouth-coating and chewy.

SCORE: 94

HOW TO DRINK: Sip.

CIGAR PAIRING: Partagas Black Label, an extremely strong cigar with a hint of coffee that latches on to this rum's coffee note for a match made in heaven.

(HAMILTON, IMPORTER) NEISSON ÉLÉVÉ SOUS BOIS, 50% ABV, MARTINIQUE

AROMA: Coffee, burnt brown sugar, maple, molasses, oak, and coffee

PALATE: Incredibly spicy, layered in toffee, dried fruit, pumpkin bread, almonds, vanilla, and hints of chocolate. Long and slightly tobacco finish.

SCORE: 90

HOW TO DRINK: If your palate can handle the heat, it's rewarding neat. But a couple of cubes of ice really make this a refreshing sipper.

CIGAR PAIRING: You want a bold cigar here. Padrón 1964's dark cocoa perfectly brings out the toffee and hint of chocolate in the rum. Great pairing!

(HAMILTON, IMPORTER) ST. LUCIA POT STILL 10-YEAR-OLD
CASK STRENGTH RUM 2004, 65.5% ABV, SAINT LUCIA

AROMA: Rounded, rich molasses. Thick and heavy. Cigar box, oak, and essential oils.

PALATE: Super big, bold, and ripe with molasses, oily, cigar, and black fruit, vanilla wafer, chocolate, and a hint of curry. It finishes long and strong with bold molasses.

SCORE: 92

HOW TO DRINK: I know this is a big rum. But damn, that flavor is intense and deserves to be sipped alone. Mix as you may, but try it alone first.

CIGAR PAIRING: La Aroma de Cuba Mi Amor Reserva Maximo. Bold meets bold.

(HAMILTON, IMPORTER) ST. LUCIA POT STILL,
46.5% ABV, SAINT LUCIA

AROMA: Baked apples, molasses cooking, earth, petrol, oak, anise, cinnamon, and eucalyptus. The alcohol is amazingly not present in this nose.

PALATE: This taste is ideal for those bourbon drinkers who love cask strength, with the backbone for the spirit's palate, and ripe with molasses, apple pie, cinnamon, and hints of tobacco and smoke. Finishes medium and warm with a taste of cane syrup.

SCORE: 88

HOW TO DRINK: Sip neat.

HAVANA CLUB 7-YEAR-OLD,
40% ABV, CUBA

AROMA: Fruit, vanilla, molasses, port, marzipan, dried apricot, smoke, extreme caramel, pomace, raisin, oak, chocolate, and citrus

PALATE: Beautiful. Caramel and orange, chocolate, cinnamon roll, blueberry pie, dried apricot, molasses, ginger, and no-bake cookie with a hint of almond butter.

SCORE: 92

HOW TO DRINK: Sip.

Located in Le François, Martinique, Habitation Clément is the birthplace of rhum agricole and still enjoys the ancient Créole sugarcane plantation culture. HOUSE OF AGRICOLE

ISAUTIER 7 ANS D'ÂGE, RHUM VIEUX,
40% ABV, RÉUNION

AROMA: If you've ever had the pleasure of taking in the aroma of cane pressing, the essence is here, with fruit, floral, oak, licorice, and hints of smoke following. The mouthwatering second sniff yields citrus, prune juice, and fresh-cut grass.

PALATE: Beautiful chewy mouthfeel, with a cadre of pome filling the palate with hints of honey, black pepper, apricot, marmalade, and a slight hint of smoke before an orange-chocolate pot de crème blossoms. It finishes long, with a lasting butterscotch taste.

SCORE: 94

HOW TO DRINK: Sip neat.

ISAUTIER RHUM LOUIS & CHARLES EDITION,
45% ABV, RÉUNION

AROMA: Reminiscent of a brandy nose, it's filled with apples, apricots, oak, leather, vanilla, and a slight hint of spice.

PALATE: It's fruit forward, with vanilla, custard, and pie crust following. A warmth overtakes the palate, offering pronounced baking spices—notably nutmeg—and a hint of coffee. A long, slightly bitter finish follows. This is the sort of rum Scotch drinkers will love, but it will turn off those conditioned to like sweetness. Despite the vanilla notes, this is fruity, not sweet.

SCORE: 97

HOW TO DRINK: Sip only. Scotch lovers will be in love with this rum.

CIGAR PAIRING: Eiroa CBT Robusto. This slow-burning cigar's sweetness and spice brings out the baking spices of the rum for a great pairing.

J. BALLY 7-YEAR-OLD RHUM VIEUX AGRICOLE MARTINIQUE,
45% ABV, MARTINIQUE

AROMA: Baked peaches, apple, gingerbread cookies coming out of the oven, with a slight hint of anise

PALATE: Very fruit forward, expressing pears, peaches, apples, citrus, and cherries. It's so fruity that you nearly miss the gorgeous chocolate and cinnamon appearing toward the end. The long finish gives a touch of vanilla.

SCORE: 89

HOW TO DRINK: Sip neat.

J. BALLY 12-YEAR-OLD,
45% ABV, MARTINIQUE

AROMA: Rose petals, oak, nuanced caramel, tobacco, cigar box, caramel, hazelnut, vanilla, and hints of citrus and spice

PALATE: Anise, caramel, vanilla, orange, rhubarb, cinnamon—really finishes bitter, with a touch of caramel

SCORE: 88

HOW TO DRINK: Sip neat.

KARUKERA RHUM VIEUX RESERVE SPECIALE,
42% ABV, GUADELOUPE

AROMA: Sugarcane, vanilla bean, leather, green coconut, and tobacco

PALATE: Oak, maple, caramel, and vanilla. It's very light on the palate at first, then the flavors strum into action. Finishes short with a hint of fruit.

SCORE: 82

HOW TO DRINK: This makes a lovely punch mixer.

MARGARITAVILLE DARK RUM,
40% ABV, CARIBBEAN

AROMA: Cough syrup, varnish, turnip juice, and slight hints of tobacco

PALATE: There's vanilla here, but in the same way vanilla extract feels on the tongue. After this, chocolate milk and rice. Finishes short.

SCORE: 60

HOW TO DRINK: If you have nothing in your cabinet for the apocalypse, then this is your dark rum floater.

MYER'S RUM ORIGINAL DARK, 40% ABV, JAMAICA

AROMA: Oak, molasses, banana bread, roasted walnuts, and molasses

PALATE: Chewy granola, molasses cookie, almonds, pear, dried apricot, and pine nut. Not classically a sipper, but it gets the job done in a pinch, with a medium finish showing a hint of cola.

SCORE: 80

HOW TO DRINK: Dark rum floater

MEZAN EXTRA OLD RUM XO JAMAICA,
40% ABV, JAMAICA

AROMA: Floral, petrol, cane juice, fruity, toasted pine nuts, alfalfa, goldenrod, honeysuckle, and pear

PALATE: Up front, pepper spice that turns into earth, and raw cane with hints of honey, peach, and strawberry jam. This is a nice rum with nothing added, and it's a great taste for a whiskey drinker.

SCORE: 85

HOW TO DRINK: While this is a worthwhile sipper, the flavor explodes when it's used in punch.

MEZAN SINGLE DISTILLERY RUM 2000,

40% ABV, JAMAICA

AROMA: Extremely rich on the nose, with sugarcane vibrant, molasses cookies, and burnt brown sugar. Hints of grass, cinnamon, and celery broth.

PALATE: Very sharp with an immediate bite, which is unwanted for such a low ABV. Then, raw molasses, sugarcane syrup, oak, spice, and hints of vanilla, fruit, and toffee. Short finish with hints of earth.

SCORE: 81

HOW TO DRINK: Punch. Recipe recommended: 1 cup Mezan, ½ cup Myer's Dark Rum, 2 cups pineapple juice, 2 cups orange juice, ½ cup lemon juice, 4 tablespoons orgeat syrup, and 1 teaspoon of pumpkin spice.

MONTANYA ORO BARREL NO. 306,

40% ABV, COLORADO, UNITED STATES

AROMA: Almost Chardonnay-like on the nose, with butter, citrus, apple, pineapple, and vanilla

PALATE: Earthy in the beginning, followed by marshmallow, grass, herbs, tropical fruits, and cinnamon over a buttery texture that is balanced and delicious. Its flaw is the short finish, with a brief hint of cola.

SCORE: 80

HOW TO DRINK: Cocktails

MONTANYA ORO BARREL NO. 327,

40% ABV, COLORADO, UNITED STATES

AROMA: Earth meets fruit. The richness in the fruit is uncanny. Black currant, orange peel, baked peaches, followed by cola and a hint of mint.

PALATE: Cherry dominates but allows in subtle caramel, honey, and spice. There's a toasted almond toward the end for a delightful medium finish.

SCORE: 82

HOW TO DRINK: Daiquiris

MONTANYA RUM EXCLUSIVA,

40% ABV, COLORADO, UNITED STATES

AROMA: Butter, toffee, honey, burnt sugar, vanilla, and oak

PALATE: For as admirable as it is on the nose, this rum's strength is in the palate, loading up on a chewy mouthfeel, with spice, caramel, dried fruit, raw almonds, honey, and malt. It finishes medium but is a great American sipper.

SCORE: 89

HOW TO DRINK: Sip.

MOUNT GAY BLACK BARREL, 43% ABV, BARBADOS

AROMA: Molasses cookies baking, ginger, caramel, vanilla, oak, leather, and cigar box

PALATE: Nuanced, balanced and ripe, with caramel, vanilla, butterscotch, citrus, cola, and fruit. Medium finish.

SCORE: 88

HOW TO DRINK: You could make a great case for Black Barrel as a sipper, but it's perfect for making cocktails. You should also taste next to other Mount Gay products for comparison.

Mount Gay is a classic Caribbean style of rum. They blend a column and aged spirit. While the distillery does not disclose its blending percentages, the pot-still nuance is detectable in all blends.

MOUNT GAY COPPER COLUMN (ORIGIN SERIES VOLUME 2),

43% ABV, BARBADOS

AROMA: This is an unimpressive nose, delivering mere hints of vanilla, licorice, and sawdust.

PALATE: Taste makes up for the bouquet. Gingerbread cookie, citrus, pear, coconut milk, caramel, and baking spices. It finishes fairly long with a hint of cinnamon.

SCORE: 86

HOW TO DRINK: Since these releases were meant to be sipped next to other Mount Gay products to discern the styles, sip next to the brand's pot still and Black Barrel for comparison.

MOUNT GAY COPPER POT (ORIGIN SERIES VOLUME 2),

43% ABV, BARBADOS

AROMA: Fresh-baked cookies, banana, pear, peach, floral, caramel, and maple

PALATE: It's gorgeous;. Feels layered upon the tongue, with light caramel, light vanilla, rich molasses cookie, baked apple, canned peaches, and hints of blackberry jam, spice, and roasted walnut.

SCORE: 90

HOW TO DRINK: Sip.

MUDDY RIVER QUEEN CHARLOTTE'S RESERVE,

42% ABV, NORTH CAROLINA, UNITED STATES

AROMA: Fresh and fruity—think cool spring day with the flowers blooming and a crispness in the air. Slight hints of cigar, honey, and maple.

PALATE: It's slightly dry but presents fruit, spice, and slight vegetal flavor that is quite pleasing. There are no off-putting flavors, as caramel and raw honey warm the palate.

SCORE: 82

HOW TO DRINK: Cocktails

Muddy River Distillery is an up-and-coming US distillery. Its Queen Charlotte is one of the better American rums.

OLD MAN GUAVABERRY BRAND,

45% ABV, SINT MAARTEN

AROMA: At first pass, this appears light on the nose, but you really need to take the time to catch the subtle fragrances wafting up in the form of floral, fruit, and molasses. A light burnt sugar appears, too, with a slight hint of vanilla. But the aroma just doesn't jump out of the glass.

PALATE: The palate comes rich and warm, with beautiful caramel, vanilla, strawberry, blueberry, and hints of tobacco plug, apple cider, and marmalade.

SCORE: 86

HOW TO DRINK: This makes an amazing punch mixer.

OPTHIMUS 25 MALT WHISKY FINISH,

40% ABV, SANTO DOMINGO, DOMINICAN REPUBLIC

AROMA: Squeezed prunes, pear, peach, hints of cinnamon, and citrus

PALATE: Gingerbread, rye bread, sugar-intense caramel, and hint of cinnamon. While these flavors are there, they're not very intense, almost muted.

SCORE: 80

HOW TO DRINK: Punch.

OPTHIMUS,

40% ABV, SANTO DOMINGO, DOMINICAN REPUBLIC

AROMA: There's a lot going on in this nose, with apricot, caramel, licorice, earth, and cigar box.

PALATE: Pumpkin, cherry pie, dried apricot, burnt crème brûlée, chocolate pot de crème, raspberry sorbet, and hints of fruit and spice. Finishes long.

SCORE: 86

HOW TO DRINK: Sip.

PARCE RUM 8-YEAR-OLD, 40 PERCENT ABV, COLOMBIA

AROMA: Burnt brown sugar, vanilla, molasses, earth, and hazelnut

PALATE: Lovely mouthfeel, velvety rich in caramel, vanilla, molasses cookie, roasted almonds, and marzipan. It's slightly sweet, but a bitter oak comes through with a hint of tobacco. Finishes long.

SCORE: 90

HOW TO DRINK: Sip neat.

CIGAR PAIRING: The CAO Colombia has a sweetness and fruitiness in a light burn, bringing out the nuttiness in the rum. Beautiful pairing.

Parce Rum 8-Year-Old.

PARCE RUM 12-YEAR-OLD,
40% ABV

AROMA: Orange zest, caramelized sugar, oak, raw pine nuts, coffee, hazelnut, and hints of fresh-cut grass and cherry blossom

PALATE: Honey, vanilla, sugarcane syrup, cinnamon, and coffee. For all its boasting flavor, the finish comes out flat—short to medium with a speck of caramel on the end.

SCORE: 85

HOW TO DRINK: Use as a mixer.

PHRAYA DEEP MATURED GOLD RUM, 40% ABV, THAILAND

AROMA: You won't find many rums with this nose. Pancake batter, coconut, maple, brown-sugar cookies, and fruit.

PALATE:: It's very expressive, with fruit, caramel, vanilla, and sweetened condensed milk. Coconut and vanilla follow this home to a medium finish. It's a coconut lover's sipping rum, for sure.

SCORE: 90

HOW TO DRINK: Sip, especially if you love coconut.

CIGAR PAIRING: Padrón 1926. Both have a maple and coconut note, making it a perfect pairing.

The Plantation rum portfolio is among the most respected and appreciated by bartenders.

PLANTATION BARBADOS 5-YEAR GRAND RESERVE,

40% ABV, BARBADOS

AROMA: Baked apple pie, molasses cookie, cherry cola, citrus, and floral

PALATE: Sweet but not overly sweet. Caramel syrup, vanilla icing, and molasses. Hints of ginger and clove.

SCORE: 86

HOW TO DRINK: This makes a beautiful cocktail enhancer.

PLANTATION 20TH ANNIVERSARY,

41.2% ABV, BARBADOS

AROMA: Ripe sugarcane, caramel, orange blossoms, daisy, rose petals, and citrus, with hints of ocean and banana

PALATE: Breathtaking mouthfeel covering every inch, from the bottom of the jawline to the roof of the mouth, complex and wonderful, tangy and sweet, with just a hint of spice. This is an extraordinary taste, with grand notes of pineapple, pear, peach, lemon curd, butterscotch, and meringue. A warm spice sits there with a long finish.

SCORE: 93

HOW TO DRINK: Sip.

CIGAR PAIRING: Nat Sherman Timeless 660. The lemon pops in the cigar and brings out the lemon curd.

PLANTATION 73% OVERPROOF, TRINIDAD AND TOBAGO

AROMA: Medicinal, grass, ocean air, chocolate, and banana

PALATE: The intensity of the heat fires up right away, but burn turns to spice and develops into ginger, caramel, vanilla, rock candy, black pepper, and a hint of maple syrup. Long and spicy finish.

SCORE: 88

HOW TO DRINK: Use for all drinks calling for overproof rum.

PLANTATION JAMAICA 2001,
42% ABV, JAMAICA

AROMA: Whoa. A rum-lover's nose. Beautiful. Raw, rich molasses, honey, clove, banana, allspice, and ginger.

PALATE: Layered in caramel, tobacco, ginger, clove, toffee, sugarcane, cinnamon, and a plethora of baking spice, with a sweetness undertone. Finishes long and strong with a hint of clove.

SCORE: 90

HOW TO DRINK: Sip neat and let it stand out in a cocktail. Either way, you'll taste it.

CIGAR PAIRING: Atabey Brujos Vitola—there's a molasses note in this cigar that explodes with a touch of rum. Or San Cristóbal de la Habana, which burns mild but has a beautiful ginger note that complements the baking spice in this rum.

PLANTATION 2002 RUM,
40% ABV, PANAMA

AROMA: This nose will be a welcome smell to whiskey drinkers, with rich notes of coffee, leather, caramel, and anise. There's a slight hint of fresh-cut grass and honey.

PALATE: It's quite sugar forward, appearing as honey and sugar in the raw, with hints of caramel and vanilla. A lovely chocolate comes toward the end in what is a decently medium finish with a hint of nutmeg.

SCORE: 86

HOW TO DRINK: Use as a mixer.

PLANTATION RUM GUYANA, DISTILLED IN 2005,
45% ABV, GUYANA

AROMA: White pepper, squeezed cane juice, lavender, pineapple, banana, and fig, with hints of grass

PALATE: Really a beautiful earthy style where you can still taste the rich and raw sugarcane juice—but complexity settles quickly, with caramel, vanilla, cinnamon, fruit, toffee, coffee, and a hint of nutmeg. It finishes long with a touch of honey.

SCORE: 90

HOW TO DRINK: Punch

CIGAR PAIRING: Pair with a heavy cigar.

PLANTATION RUM ORIGINAL DARK, 40% ABV, TRINIDAD

AROMA: Wow, this is an array of aroma, from tobacco, baked peach, cinnamon, baked apple, and sliced pineapple.

PALATE: Fruit and spice becomes peach cobbler with nutmeg and cinnamon. Then, a brown-sugar butter, followed by caramel and vanilla.

SCORE: 89

HOW TO DRINK: Cocktails

PUERTO ANGEL AMBER, 40% ABV, MEXICO

AROMA: Raw cane, sorghum syrup, rhubarb, oak, brown sugar, and cinnamon

PALATE: The cane's essence is here, rich and full bodied, earthy with subtle sweetness in the form of agave syrup, caramel, and vanilla, with a hint of maple syrup. Pepper spice explodes toward the end, mingling with the cane's natural sweetness and earthiness.

SCORE: 90

HOW TO DRINK: This is a fun sipper, but you must like earth. If you don't, mix this in punch and you'll be rewarded with flavor.

CIGAR PAIRING: Oddly, I've found that really cheap cigars pair nicely with this rum. Swisher Sweets' vanilla brings out the vanilla in Puerto Angel Amber.

PUSSER'S GUNPOWDER,

54.5% ABV, CARIBBEAN

AROMA: Ripe with tobacco, leather over alcohol, and oak undertones

PALATE: Honey, coffee, burnt toast, chewing tobacco, cigar, and heavy molasses. A little water makes this an approachable sipper, but it's quite appealing in punches and cocktails as is.

SCORE: 78

HOW TO DRINK: Cocktails

RANK WILDCAT BLACK GOLD,

40% ABV, LOUISIANA, UNITED STATES

AROMA: Chocolate, oak, pipe tobacco, vanilla, followed by tobacco smoke and honey

PALATE: It's worth noting that this rum is clean and without technical flaws. Charming coffee, tobacco, and vanilla offer simple pleasures. The short finish gives a slight hint of malt. It's a lovely rum with much potential.

SCORE: 78

HOW TO DRINK: Cocktails. This rum could immediately become a well mixer for any major bar.

THE REAL MCCOY 3-YEAR-OLD, 40% ABV, BARBADOS

AROMA: Slight hints of ginger, molasses, and pear

PALATE: By design, this is not meant to be a sipper, but it offers a sipper's chance with coconut, gingerbread, caramel, spice, and almond. But its ideal use is in a cocktail.

SCORE: 80

HOW TO DRINK: Daiquiri

THE BAHAMA QUEEN

THE REAL MCCOY 5-YEAR-OLD, 40% ABV, BARBADOS

AROMA: Toffee, butterscotch, baked bread, and hints of chocolate

PALATE: Structure-wise, it feels beautiful—perfectly coating the palate with brown sugar, butter, ginger, baked peaches, cinnamon, and allspice. The rum's flaw is in the finish—a very short finish considering the pronounced flavor in the palate.

SCORE: 81

HOW TO DRINK: Cocktails

THE REAL MCCOY 12-YEAR-OLD, 40% ABV, BARBADOS

AROMA: Nuanced caramel, gingerbread, baked apples, toffee, coffee, mint, and a hint of earth

PALATE: Right away, vanilla and lots of it, but it's a soft approach, with hints of fruit and spice. Dulled caramel, marshmallow, and peach cobbler over a slight hint of smoke and herbs.

SCORE: 86

HOW TO DRINK: Sip.

THE REAL MCCOY LIMITED EDITION RUM, MADEIRA & BOURBON CASKS, 12 YEARS, 46% ABV, BARBADOS

AROMA: Gingerbread cookies fresh out of the oven, vanilla, caramel, cherries, dark fruit, hints of clove, molasses, and oak

PALATE: Richness and layers upon layers sit on this velvety mouthfeel. So creamy, so elegant, and so complex. Roasted almonds, baking spices, butterscotch, brown sugar, burnt cinnamon roll, almond butter, hints of coconut, and citrus. The long and spicy finish is quite enjoyable.

SCORE: 96

HOW TO DRINK: Sip only.

CIGAR PAIRING: Mayimbe by A. J. Fernandez offers a lovely full-bodied approach with a hint of gingerbread that really pops with a taste of this rum.

OPPOSITE: *The Real McCoy Rum is produced at Foursquare Distillery in Barbados but is owned by filmmaker Bailey Pryor, producer of the film* The Real McCoy.

RHUM BARBANCOURT 8-YEAR-OLD 5 STAR,
40% ABV, HAITI

AROMA: Sawdust, straw, smoldering wood, and bright floral over hints of coffee and hazelnut, with slight hints of vanilla and oak

PALATE: This is an interesting herbal taste, with hints of vanilla, caramel, pine nut, and cinnamon. A chocolate note comes toward the end that consumes the palate, warm and long for a lovely finish.

SCORE: 90

HOW TO DRINK: Sip.

CIGAR PAIRING: Romeo y Julieta Reserve Maduro. Hello, chocolate explosion. This pairing screams chocolate.

RHUM BARBANCOURT 15-YEAR-OLD, 40% ABV, HAITI

AROMA: Molasses, coffee, vanilla, oak, turmeric, and earth

PALATE: Chocolate, hazelnut, toffee, condensed milk, and hints of fruit—and nice pepper spices coating the palate. A second pour shows delicate baking spices with hints of ginger, candied orange, and rich caramel. It finishes long, with spice.

SCORE: 92

HOW TO DRINK: Sip only. If you attempt to mix this, the Haitian people will find you.

CIGAR PAIRING: Fonseca Cosacos burns medium and has a beautiful orange zest that brings out the candied orange in this 15-year-old rum.

RHUM DEPAZ VSOP, 45% ABV, MARTINIQUE

AROMA: Fruit, oak, chocolate, tobacco, cola, orange soda, and earth

PALATE: Honey, bubble gum, vanilla, strawberry, orange, and baking spice. However, it lacks balance. The bubble gum note persists, masking much of this rum. But the backbone would make it a great rum cocktail mixer.

SCORE: 76

HOW TO DRINK: Cocktails

RHUM DEPAZ XO, 45% ABV, MARTINIQUE

AROMA: A Scotch-oriented nose, especially if you're acquainted with Speyside. It's balanced, with sweet, spice, a hint of smoke, and an overwhelming fruit, with hints of leather and citrus.

PALATE: From Scotch to brandy, it yet again mimics another spirit, but nothing could be a greater compliment than to be so delicious you can't even identify the spirit. It's just delicious. Honey, caramel in several ideations, fruit, dried apricot, and blackberry jam over a subtle hint of smoke. It finishes shorter than the fabulous taste might suggest.

SCORE: 90

HOW TO DRINK: This is a sipper with a long finish.

CIGAR PAIRING: Something with a long vanilla finish.

RHUM JM GOLD,
50% ABV, MARTINIQUE

AROMA: When earth meets rich baking spices and caramel, that's a fine nose. Hints of leather, oak, and cigar box, followed by vanilla and fruit.

PALATE: Spice comes early and often in forms of baking spices and pepper spices, then pronounced sugarcane juice with a hint of caramel. Finishes medium and spicy.

SCORE: 84

HOW TO DRINK: This works great in cocktails.

While it may seem sacrilegious to many, mixing with higher-end rums can be incredibly rewarding. There are some that should be off the table, such as Foursquare 2006 and Hamilton St. Lucia French Oak, but the upper middle tier like Depaz XO will reward a thirsty palate looking for premium rum flavor.

RHUM JM V.O., 50% ABV, MARTINIQUE

AROMA: Think fruit and lots of it. Cherries, peaches, plum, apple and pear, followed by honey and vanilla.

FLAVOR: Slight anise with chocolate, sharp cinnamon and vanilla, with a medium to long finish that offers a warm taste of honey

SCORE: 88

HOW TO DRINK: Sip.

RHUM NEGRITA, 37.5% ABV, CARIBBEAN

AROMA: Oak, pine, light caramel, vanilla, molasses, earth, and no-bake cookies

PALATE: Very light in caramel and vanilla, but with a slight chocolate on the end with a touch of tobacco. It's a short finish.

SCORE: 80

HOW TO DRINK: Cocktails

RICHLAND RUM SINGLE BARREL,

43% ABV, GEORGIA, UNITED STATES

AROMA: Rich oak, caramel, chocolate, tobacco, and leather, with hints of anise, oregano, and cola

PALATE: Warm and fruity right away, with slight caramel coming in and quickly becoming a chocolate-caramel-tart note. There's an espresso bitterness toward the end, with a touch of hazelnut and toffee. Finishes long with a lovely tobacco note.

SCORE: 94

HOW TO DRINK: Sip.

CIGAR PAIRING: Due to the strong tobacco notes here, you'll find many medium-bodied cigars that pair beautifully.

Single-barrel is an overused term and may not even mean single barrel. But Richland Rum is truly only bottling single-barrel rum, an ode to the American way.

RON ABUELO 7-YEAR-OLD,

40% ABV, PANAMA

AROMA: Cherrywood, chocolate, vanilla, leather, and a hint of clove and caramel

PALATE: Coffee, vanilla, cocoa, tobacco, and slight hints of hazelnut and brown sugar

SCORE: 84

HOW TO DRINK: This is a solid sipper but lacks complexity to make the top tier. On the cocktail front, however, look for dark rum recipes.

RON ABUELO 10-YEAR-OLD AÑEJO,

45% ABV, PANAMA

AROMA: This is a sweet nose, with torched brown sugar, confectionary sugar, strawberry, and vanilla, balanced only by hints of coffee and oak.

PALATE: Given that the nose was so sweet, I was a little worried this would be a sugar bomb, but it's not. While vanilla and sweetness have the edge over spice, the fruit, chocolate, oats, anise, and spice are prevalent enough to strike balance. It finishes strong, with a note of butterscotch.

SCORE: 85

HOW TO DRINK: This is a rum many would classify as among the best. I do not think this is Ron Abuelo's best rum, but it's a noted sipper if you love sweeter styles.

RON ABUELO 12-YEAR-OLD,

40% ABV, PANAMA

AROMA: There's a really pronounced coffee note that is followed by caramel, melting butter, burnt brown sugar, and hazelnut.

PALATE: Think butter with a dab of brown sugar, a quick blast of vanilla, green apple, cherry with hints of hazelnut and almond. Medium finish is sweet.

SCORE: 86

HOW TO DRINK: Add to your morning coffee when the boss isn't looking.

RON ABUELO AÑEJO OLOROSO SHERRY CASK,

40%T ABV, PANAMA

AROMA: Dried apricot, roasted nuts, marzipan, vanilla, chocolate, and caramel

PALATE: Very sherry forward, with dried fruits and nuts, but the molasses comes through, delivering a few sugar cookie and chocolate notes. However, the nuttiness dominates this in a beautiful way.

SCORE: 90

HOW TO DRINK: If you love nuts, you'll love this as a sipper.

CIGAR PAIRING: D'Crossier Golden Blend. The pairing is an apricot delight.

RON ABUELO CENTURIA,

40% ABV, PANAMA

AROMA: Burnt sugar, toffee, coffee, oak, cigar box, leather, vanilla, crème brûlée, and a distant hint of campfire smoke

PALATE: An array of caramelized sugars blast through, followed by hazelnut, coffee, coconut, marzipan, port, dried apricot, and lingering nutmeg, with a hint of cinnamon on the finish.

SCORE: 88

HOW TO DRINK: This feels like cognac on the palate—so if you like cognac, it's a must-have sipper. Otherwise, enjoy in citrus-forward cocktails.

RON ABUELO VARELA XV OLOROSO SHERRY CASK FINISH,

40% ABV, PANAMA

AROMA: Oh boy, an explosion of aromas in the glass. Cherry, vanilla, fresh-cut cucumber, out-of-the-oven sugar cookies, and baked nuts.

PALATE: It's nutty, with hints of vanilla, molasses cookie dough, ginger, nutmeg, baked apples, and cinnamon, with a long, spicy finish and slight hint of cherry cola.

SCORE: 92

HOW TO DRINK: Sip neat.

CIGAR PAIRING: Nestor Miranda Grand Reserve 2012 offers a dark-cherry note that really complements the hints of cherry in this rum.

RON ABUELO XV NAPOLEON COGNAC CASKS,

40% ABV, PANAMA

AROMA: Nuanced vanilla, caramel, cinnamon, and hints of molasses, cornbread cooking, and raisins

PALATE: Brown sugar, toffee, and molasses. This is really light and sweet but never really comes to fruition with balance. Short finish.

SCORE: 82

HOW TO DRINK: I really want to recommend this as a sipper because its initial qualities are there, but it lacks the nuance and complexity to make it past the cocktail shaker. You'll find it's a decent cocktail mixer, especially for citrus-forward drinks.

RON CARTAVIO SELECTO RUM 5-YEAR-OLD,

40% ABV, PERU

AROMA: Cherry cola, vanilla, chocolate, nutmeg, and oak

PALATE: Soft and light with notes of fruit and caramel

SCORE: 80

HOW TO DRINK: Consider this for the lead rum in all cocktails calling for aged rum.

RON CARTAVIO SOLERA 12-YEAR-OLD,

40% ABV, PERU

AROMA: Melting butter, brown sugar, vanilla extract, white pepper, mint, and a hint of cherry medicinal

PALATE: Bright and up-front spice, with caramel nuance and vanilla notes following. Cinnamon, molasses sugar cookie, and buttercream. Beautiful, mouth-coating mouthfeel all the way until the finish, where a lovely nutmeg brings it home.

SCORE: 92

HOW TO DRINK: Sipper or cocktails.

CIGAR PAIRING: Ave Maria Barbarossa. There's a nuttiness in this burn that complements and cuts the sweetness in the rum.

RON CARTAVIO XO, 40% ABV, PERU

AROMA: Brown sugar, coffee, vibrant vanilla, rich butterscotch, layered caramel, tobacco, leather, and mink oil

PALATE: From the moment it touches your tongue, it sends flavors from the tip all the way to the back, coating every inch with notes of hazelnut syrup, caramel, Arabica coffee, toffee, and dark chocolate. The second taste brings out berry fruit and pome. Finishes long and sweet.

SCORE: 95

HOW TO DRINK: Sip only. This skews slightly sweet, so if you're a lover of the sweet, it's a must-have sipper.

CIGAR PAIRING: Avo XO. The wood and nuttiness brings out Cartavio XO's hazelnut qualities. It's a match made in heaven.

RON DURAN, 40% ABV, PANAMA

AROMA: Chocolate, buttered popcorn, vanilla, fruit, and caramel

PALATE: Soft mouthfeel with subtle caramel, almond, cashew butter, brown sugar, and pumpkin pie over extremely pronounced apple, peach, and pear. Then hints of rhubarb and cinnamon. Medium finish with a hint of vanilla. There's a velvety aspect to this rum, which you don't expect when a puncher's fist is on the label.

SCORE: 90

HOW TO DRINK: Sip.

CIGAR PAIRING: Nat Sherman 314. Its vanilla complements the rich vanilla from the rum.

Ron Duran rum pairs beautifully with Nat Sherman. It's as if these two companies collaborated to create complementary flavors.

RON FRANCISCO MONTERO 50TH ANNIVERSARY,
40% ABV, SPAIN

AROMA: Apple, cinnamon, cherry, molasses, pineapple, honeysuckle, rose petal, pine, and hints of caramel

PALATE: Strong on the apple, from the peel to a baked apple pie. Molasses sugar cookie, honey, vanilla, cherry pie, and caramel. Decent finish with a cinnamon-sprinkled green apple.

SCORE: 88

HOW TO DRINK: Sip.

RON MONTERO GRAN RESERVA, **40% ABV, SPAIN**

AROMA: Oak, almonds, coffee, vanilla, and campfire smoke

PALATE: Gorgeous spice and fruit up front. Then citrus, roasted walnuts, and coffee, followed by a bitterness. Finishes medium, with a hint of oak.

SCORE: 80

HOW TO DRINK: Cocktails

RON MULATA 5-YEAR-OLD,
38% ABV, CUBA

AROMA: Very interesting. A mix of sour and herbal qualities right off the top. Think green apple, lemon and lime, followed by herbs, fresh-cut grass, and mushrooms. Followed by hints of molasses and oak.

PALATE: The taste sways from the earth to more of a sweet, with vanilla and light caramel over an oily mouthfeel. From here, gingerbread and cola with a gentle earth undertone. It finishes with a hint of chocolate.

SCORE: 90

HOW TO DRINK: This is a sipper for sure.

RON PALIDO,
40% ABV, SPAIN

AROMA: Floral, fruit, and caramel

PALATE: Powerful alcohol notes up front, softening with touches of oak, caramel, and apple coming forward. Slightly astringent, with a short finish.

SCORE: 60

HOW TO DRINK: Consider using this in drinks calling for vodka.

RON SANTERO 7-YEAR-OLD,

38% ABV, CUBA

AROMA: Almond butter, molasses, pineapple, dark chocolate, apple butter, fresh-baked croissant, leather, and oak

PALATE: Black licorice, tobacco, vanilla, oak, mint, dark chocolate, hazelnut, walnut shell, and a hint of nutmeg. The medium finish presents a short burst of dried apple.

SCORE: 88

HOW TO DRINK: This rum is a must-have sipper if you love bitter. The licorice, tobacco, and walnut shell are very enticing. If these notes are not for you, then look at this for all cocktails.

RON SANTERO AÑEJO RESERVA,

38% ABV, CUBA

AROMA: Green apple, light molasses, oats, dried apricot, canned peaches, and black fruit

PALATE: Although this rum is light in weight, it covers every inch of the palate with intense spice, vanilla, caramel chew, apple, pineapple, raw almonds, and honey. The extremely long finish allows for complexity to develop with a slight hint of ginger.

SCORE: 94

HOW TO DRINK: Because this packs so much flavor with so little proof, I do not recommend diluting. You may lose the flavor with water, ice, or in cocktails. So, this is for sipping only.

RON SANTIAGO AÑEJO,

38% ABV, CUBA

AROMA: An extremely intense and layered nose with coffee, vanilla, molasses, caramel, yeast roll, baked pecan, peach preserves, cigar box, brown sugar, tobacco, and a slight hint of banana

PALATE: Extraordinarily complex with vanilla, caramel, crème brûlée, chocolate, cinnamon, oak, slight hints of smoke, marzipan, baked apple pie, burnt brown sugar, and a long finish with a hint of cinnamon

SCORE: 97

HOW TO DRINK: Sip neat. Under no circumstances should this rum be diluted.

RON ZACAPA 23 SOLERA,

40% ABV, GUATEMALA

AROMA: Brown sugar, torched white sugar, caramel, vanilla, mint, pear, and apple

PALATE: Texturally, sweet overpowers the mouthfeel and gives a sugar-packet-like flavor profile that disappoints.

SCORE: 82

HOW TO DRINK: Use in cocktails calling for sugar, but hold the sugar. The rum will keep the drink sweet.

RUM-BAR GOLD, WORTHY ESTATE,

40% ABV, JAMAICA

AROMA: Spearmint, rhubarb, vanilla, and pine

PALATE: It's clean, definitely offering a balanced taste of cane, spice, and herbs. But it falls slightly flat and lacks nuance to be more than a cocktail mixer.

SCORE: 79

HOW TO DRINK: Daiquiri

RUMSON'S, 40% ABV, TRINIDAD AND TOBAGO

AROMA: Cola, burnt sugar, eucalyptus, burnt plastic, and vanilla

PALATE: Sugar, mint, basil, bubble gum, cherry cola, and caramel

SCORE: 65

HOW TO DRINK: Rum and Coke

ST. GEORGE CALIFORNIA RESERVE AGRICOLE RUM,

40% ABV, CALIFORNIA, UNITED STATES

AROMA: After the raw funk from the sugarcane, there's a Southern baking shop, with gingerbread and baked apples over maple, vanilla, and torched brown sugar

PALATE: There's a gorgeous mouthfeel here, coating the palate with molasses, apples, pears, pineapple, cinnamon, nutmeg, and lovely raw cane toward the end. Finishes long and rich with molasses.

SCORE: 92

HOW TO DRINK: If you love funk, this is your Monday-night sipper.

CIGAR PAIRING: Look for extremely bold cigars to cut through the rich molasses.

SAINT JAMES RHUM VIEUX AGRICOLE, 42% ABV, MARTINIQUE

AROMA: As is the case with most Martinique rums, this nose walks the imposter line of part brandy, part sherry, part Scotch nose. But a closer whiff will detect the origins—the beautiful sugarcane in full representative form, followed by perfume-like fruits, floral, and caramel.

PALATE: Right away, the palate meets a flavorful rum that delivers an assortment of fruit in dried, raw, and cooked form. Think dried peach, then raw peach and peach cobbler. Then delicate spice in baking spice form, such as cinnamon, and peppers, specifically cayenne. It finishes with a touch of caramel on a long and lasting taste.

SCORE: 88

HOW TO DRINK: Very nice sipper, but it makes a beautiful rum Brown Derby: 2 ounces Saint James, 1 ounce freshly squeezed grapefruit juice, and ½ ounce honey syrup.

SAINT LUCIA CHAIRMAN'S RESERVE, 40% ABV, SAINT LUCIA

AROMA: Extremely vibrant, with cinnamon, vanilla, crushed dark cherries, baked apples, and caramel

PALATE: The vibrancy continues, tickling every inch with chocolate-chip cookie dough, vanilla, raspberry, banana, and swooshing caramel chew that lingers until a gorgeous, cinnamon-dusted apple finishes and lasts for a lovely long time.

SCORE: 90

HOW TO DRINK: Sip.

CIGAR PAIRING: Pair with a medium-bodied cigar.

ST. NICHOLAS ABBEY 5-YEAR-OLD, 40% ABV, BARBADOS

AROMA: Sweet meets earth, a range of caramel, vanilla as well as coconut husk, grass, fresh-baked sugar cookies, and oatmeal cookies, with resounding layers of chocolate

PALATE: The chocolate continues with milk stout, caramel, vanilla, almond butter, and pecan shell. Decent finish with a hint of mint.

SCORE: 86

HOW TO DRINK: The thickness of this rum makes for a lovely add to coffee or hot chocolate.

OPPOSITE: *In Saint Peter, Barbados, is the historic plantation house and museum St. Nicholas Abbey. Built in 1658 by Col. Benjamin Berringer, it's one of only three Jacobean mansions in the Western Hemisphere. The rum isn't bad either.*

ST. NICHOLAS ABBEY 12-YEAR-OLD,

40% ABV, BARBADOS

AROMA: This nose walks the line of complex and different. Filled with fruit, vanilla, fresh-baked sugar cookies, citrus, leather, cigar box, and hints of chocolate, the notes are many, tickling the nose with the same delicacy as the perfect perfume

PALATE: The complexity continues. Marzipan, chocolate, coconut, pecan shell, butternut squash, vanilla, caramel chew, glazed donut, and pineapple over a chewy mouthfeel, with a long finish with just a hint of coconut.

SCORE: 94

HOW TO DRINK: Sip only.

CIGAR PAIRING: Ramón Allones Specially Selected. The marzipan in both brings out the beauty of each.

SMOOTH AMBLER REVELATION RUM,

47.4% ABV, JAMAICA

AROMA: Floral, fruit, caramel, vanilla, toffee, honey, and maraschino cherries

PALATE: This is rum at its finest. The spirit trickles down the jawline, filling it with spice, molasses, caramel, vanilla, nutmeg, and fruit. The long and lasting finish lingers, giving a beautiful graham cracker taste. Its only flaw is that the flavors feel lighter during the taste, but this is made up with a wonderful finish.

SCORE: 89

HOW TO DRINK: This feels light for a Jamaican rum, but it's still sip worthy.

SMOOTH AMBLER REVELATION RUM RYE CASK FINISH,

49.5% ABV, JAMAICA

AROMA: Cotton candy, red fruit, vanilla, caramel, cinnamon, nutmeg, leather, cigar box, and a hint of toasted walnut

PALATE: On the palate, many could taste this and think it's a whiskey. The rye cask really bolstered this flavor profile. It's loaded with spice, with hints of toasted rye bread, caramel, vanilla, and a slight hint of mint. Rye whiskey drinkers will love this.

SCORE: 82

HOW TO DRINK: American whiskey drinkers will love this because of the rye-centric spice notes.

SOUTH BAY SMALL BATCH 18,

40% ABV, DOMINICAN REPUBLIC

AROMA: Sugar caramelizing in a pan with butter, vanilla, and hints of mint

PALATE: Sweet crisp apple, toffee, caramel, and a touch of cinnamon. The short finish leaves much to be desired.

SCORE: 75

HOW TO DRINK: This rum's best use is in cocktails calling for sugar. Instead of adding sugar, however, just use this rum.

TAILDRAGGER DARK RUM,

57.5% ABV, ILLINOIS, UNITED STATES

AROMA: Freshly opened bag of confectionary sugar and popped corn, with notes of toffee, caramel, vanilla, coffee, and burnt butter

PALATE: From an alcohol-percentage standpoint, this rum is right on the money at 115 proof. The higher proof helps balance the sweetness and gives it a subtle balance with spice, caramel, and vanilla, with hints of maple syrup, roasted almonds, marzipan, and strawberry jam. It finishes strong, with a slight hint of apple butter.

SCORE: 86

HOW TO DRINK: High-proof cocktails

TORTUGA 12-YEAR-OLD,

40% ABV, CARIBBEAN

AROMA: Vibrant vanilla, caramel, and tree fruit—especially banana—and pineapple, with hints of honey, brown butter, and baked wheat bread

PALATE: There's definitely an overriding sweetness here, but it becomes balanced with pear, peach, and a hint of ginger. This would be an excellent cocktail mixer.

SCORE: 80

HOW TO DRINK: Mix with ginger ale or use in punch.

TORTUGA PREMIUM GOLD RUM 5-YEAR-OLD,

40% ABV, CARIBBEAN

AROMA: A French pastry room, with loads of vanilla, sugarcane, Southern garden, herbs, cinnamon, pepper, and fresh-cut grass

When it comes to finding the perfect rum for a cocktail, the basic idea is that if you want to taste the rum, you go with the aged rums or an agricole. If you're just adding it to cola, you're in less of a need for an aged rum.

PALATE: Light but velvety, with brown sugar and maple syrup, followed by gingerbread, nutmeg, and pumpkin. It's an interesting taste, walking the line of sweet but not too sweet.

SCORE: 88

HOW TO DRINK: Cocktails

TRES HOMBRES VIII ANS D'ÂGE AGRICOLE, 44% ABV

AROMA: Vanilla, straw, herbs, anise, and tobacco

PALATE: Sharp oak and bitterness with medicinal undertones, followed by a sweeter red licorice, caramel, and oregano. Finishes medium with oak.

SCORE: 80

HOW TO DRINK: If you like bitterness, this is a must-have sipper. Otherwise, it would make a great Sazerac or other rye-whiskey-leaning cocktail.

TRES HOMBRES VIII EDITION 14 8-YEAR-OLD, MARIE GALANTE RHUM AGRICOLE VIEUX, 55% ABV

AROMA: This is an amazing nose, filled with vanilla, cotton candy, caramel, hints of cane juice, and oak. Slight hints of apple, leather, and grass.

PALATE: Pure bliss for the spirits drinker. If you love the feel of a high-proof yet balanced spirit upon your palate, this is for you. Loaded with banana, pineapple, plum, honey, caramel, and a blast of baking spices that bring you home for a beautiful long finish. This rum's only flaw is it lacks supreme balance—but if you love the notes described, you may consider this flawless.

SCORE: 93

HOW TO DRINK: Sip.

CIGAR PAIRING: Bandolero. A pairing of baking-spice delight.

TRES HOMBRES XVIII, SOLERA, DOMINICAN REPUBLIC, EDITION 15, 43.1% ABV

AROMA: Herbal, medicinal, licorice, oak, apple, and burnt sugar

PALATE: It hits with a sweetness early and often, but sandwiched in between sugar cookie and cane syrup with extra sugar are delicious fruits, spices, and nuts.

SCORE: 80

HOW TO DRINK: Cocktails

TRES HOMBRES FAIRTRANSPORT RUM, VIII YEARS AGED, BARBADOS OLD RUM, 41.3% ABV

AROMA: Gorgeous. Vanilla, caramel, melted white chocolate, marshmallow, oak, leather, fresh cream being whipped, orange peel, coconut, and a touch of spice.

PALATE: The palate picks up where the nose left, offering more pronounced versions, such as vanilla becoming a custard, caramel into salted caramel, white chocolate into a white chocolate pretzel, as well as robust coconut and buttery goodness throughout. This finishes long and strong with a hint of baking spice.

SCORE: 96

HOW TO DRINK: Sip only. If I discover you used this in a cocktail, I will hire mercenaries to hunt you down and take your bottle away.

CIGAR PAIRING: Viaje Exclusivo. A delicious combination and a lovely salt comes through with a hint of powerful cinnamon in the pairing.

TRES HOMBRES FAIRTRANSPORT RUM RON JOVEN, LA PALMA BLANCO, 40.4% ABV

AROMA: Raw, herbal, vegetal, swamp, smoke, and tomato juice

PALATE: Very light-bodied, but prominent herbal, vegetal, and light spice notes. Finishes quickly with a slight burst of tamale. This is a unique rum.

SCORE: 80

HOW TO DRINK: Use in cocktails looking for a very interesting base spirit.

TRES HOMBRES LA PALMA ORO, 42.2% ABV

AROMA: Chocolate, oak, berries, vanilla, and a hint of molasses

PALATE: Rich and complex, with beautiful caramel, vanilla, baking spice (especially nutmeg), hazelnut, dried apricot, citrus, and a hint of tobacco. Finishes long with a hint of caramel.

SCORE: 89

HOW TO DRINK: This is an ideal sipper but should also be considered for cocktails calling for well-aged rum.

CHAPTER 6

FLAVORED RUM

IF YOU OR SOMEBODY YOU KNOW ENJOYS FLAVORED RUM, this is your section. I generally don't care for flavored spirits, but some flavored rums have a nice artisanal quality, while others are just added chemicals.

What I'm looking for: In spirits that have flavor added, there are several ways the flavor can be added. Some have food chemicals added. Others are macerated. In either case, you must not taste the chemical. Anything that tastes like a chemistry lab concoction will receive low scores from me, although they may certainly be fine mixed with cola. After evaluating the chemical nature, I look for its sipping quality. Can I taste the base ingredient? In flavored rums, there's sometimes a chance one will be an enjoyable sipper.

Flavored rum is beloved by many, and mainstream consumers often believe spiced rum to be superior to aged rums. With that said, the category is all over the place, and some, such as Guavaberry, are in fact liqueurs.

BAYOU SATSUMA RUM LIQUEUR,

30% ABV, LOUISIANA, UNITED STATES

AROMA: Orange juice, orange peel, orange marmalade, and orange powder mix

PALATE: This is an extremely balanced liqueur, with taste of the rum showing and strong hints of orange peel. This may be an interesting mixer for sidecars and cocktails that call for orange liqueurs. As a sipper, it brings orange, slight hints of cinnamon, and sugar cookie.

SCORE: 80

HOW TO DRINK: This makes a decent replacement for cocktails calling for triple sec.

BAYOU SPICED RUM,

40% ABV, LOUISIANA, UNITED STATES

AROMA: Distinctly rum forward, with delicate spice presenting itself, followed by fruit and oak

PALATE: Rum notes of molasses and caramel come first, then subtle spice tickles the palate. It's extremely soft and a decent sipper.

SCORE: 79

HOW TO DRINK: With cola, if you wouldn't mind a spicy Rum and Coke.

BLACK MAGIC SPICED,

47% ABV, IMPORTED FROM UNKNOWN ORIGIN

AROMA: Cola, boiling sugar water, and molasses

PALATE: This is an exceptionally rich and very flavorful spicy rum with notes of nutmeg, cinnamon, chocolate, and vanilla. No impurities or chemical mouthfeels overtake the notes. Nonetheless, it's a simple taste, meant for just that.

SCORE: 80

HOW TO DRINK:

BOUKMAN BOTANICAL RHUM, 45% ABV, HAITI

AROMA: This is a beautiful rum with hints of citrus, earth, cinnamon, honey, and baked pear.

PALATE: First a beautiful spice, almost like jerk spice, then wood, chocolate, fruit, molasses, and key-lime pie. It finishes long and slightly medicinal with spice.

SCORE: 92

HOW TO DRINK: Sip if you love spice and herbs. It's quite splendid.

CHAIRMAN'S RESERVE SPICED,

40% ABV, SAINT LUCIA

AROMA: Bubble gum, cola, clove, and rhubarb

PALATE: Think cinnamon maple syrup with a touch of cherry. For a flavored rum, it certainly has the flavor.

SCORE: 78

HOW TO DRINK: This makes a great additive in a whiskey cocktail.

CHEF DISTILLED GREEN COCONUT,

40% ABV, FLORIDA, UNITED STATES

AROMA: Coconut, tree bark

PALATE: The coconut flavor doesn't really hit as hard as you'd think considering the nose. It's softer on approach and comes in fast toward the finish. But the flavor is pure coconut, almost like you're cracking open and eating a fresh one from the tree.

SCORE: 79

HOW TO DRINK: Believe it or not, this makes an amazing Rum and Coke with a lime spritz.

CHEF DISTILLED KEY LIME

40% ABV, FLORIDA, UNITED STATES

AROMA: Lime

PALATE: Very tart, rich with lime and other citrus. No oversugared undertones as is often found in flavored rums such as this. It's really authentic and greatly tastes like a key lime pie.

SCORE: 80

HOW TO DRINK: If you love key lime pie, just sip it neat.

COCKSPUR SPICED RUM,

22% ABV, BARBADOS

AROMA: Think the scents of a holiday store: cinnamon sticks, gingerbread cookies, nutmeg dusted over a pumpkin pie. It's all here and then some, with vanilla and molasses making a brief appearance.

PALATE: Soft and velvety with cardamom, ginger, and cinnamon

SCORE: 89

HOW TO DRINK: Pour in your eggnog, sit back, and chill by the fire.

Cinnamon is a common flavoring agent for spiced rums.

FAMILLE OKSEN BANANE (BANANA),

40% ABV, FRANCE

AROMA: Imagine the creation of bananas Foster or banana bread, the slow cooking, and the nuts, banana, and sugar notes just filling the air. That's what's here, and it's delightful.

PALATE: This is just gorgeous. If you're a banana lover, buy a case or six. It's not sweet or laden in chemical notes. It's a pure infusion trip of rich banana in the cooked form, with caramel syrup and baking spices. Finishes strong with (you guessed it) banana. Great to sip as an aperitif or to mix for the banana lover.

SCORE: 90

HOW TO DRINK: As an apértif

FAMILLE OKSEN BÂTON DE CANNELLE,

40% ABV, FRANCE

AROMA: Many forms of cinnamon, ranging from straight from the baking spice cabinet to rising cinnamon rolls. There are also hints of pecan, toasted almond, and molasses cookie baking in the oven.

PALATE: Look out, Fireball whiskey—this is the best cinnamon-flavored spirit in the world. But it's for a connoisseur, not the shot market. This is layered in cinnamon obviously, with true rum appearing just behind the intended flavoring. Hints of baked apple, green apple, citrus, and cane juice jump out just before a long and lasting cinnamon finish.

SCORE: 92

HOW TO DRINK: Sip.

FAMILLE OKSEN SPICED RUM (ORANGE),

40% ABV, FRANCE

AROMA: Beautiful and powerful orange peel, cinnamon, and lemon zest

PALATE: Spice, chocolate, and a Chinese-style pan-sautéed orange peel. However, these notes are very pungent and unbalanced. Astringent toward the end.

SCORE: 70

HOW TO DRINK: If you love orange, sip.

FOURSQUARE SPICED RUM,

35% ABV, BARBADOS

AROMA: Coffee, cola, cherries, and toffee

PALATE: Very cola forward, with hints of vanilla, clove, and butterscotch. Finishes short, but it's not meant to be a sipper.

SCORE: 72

HOW TO DRINK: With cola

HAMILTON PIMENTO DRAM,

30% ABV, JAMAICA

AROMA: Clove, allspice, Chinese allspice, crushed jalapeños, ginger, and nutmeg

PALATE: Beautiful. If you love a baking spice rack and all the nutmeg, clove, and allspice you can imagine, this is your dream taste. There's nothing like this in the world. It's spectacular.

SCORE: 95

HOW TO DRINK: Sip it as an after-dinner drink, use it as a base for low-alcohol cocktails, or make it the amplifier mixer for a drink. But buy this and use it. A lot.

KEY WEST SPICED,

40% ABV, FLORIDA, UNITED STATES

AROMA: Clove, cardamom, and cinnamom

PALATE: When assessing Key West and the spiced rums that follow, evaluating requires an open mind. These are not real rums but flavored rums. In Key West Spiced, we find clove in heavy doses, followed by nutmeg and pumpkin. It has all the flavors for a Halloween drink.

SCORE: 79

HOW TO DRINK: Punch

MARGARITAVILLE COCONUT RUM,

21% ABV, CARIBBEAN

AROMA: Freshly cracked coconut, pan-frying coconut oil and nuts

PALATE: It's obviously coconut but doesn't taste artificial. At this proof, you don't expect to taste rum, but a hint of molasses comes toward the end.

SCORE: 70

HOW TO DRINK: This would make an excellent secondary spirit in a cocktail or could be used in a piña colada.

MARGARITAVILLE SPICED RUM,

35% ABV, CARIBBEAN

AROMA: Clove and peppermint

PALATE: Easy sipping, with a really enticing vanilla note. But even though it's a flavored rum, I expect more than a one-note wonder.

SCORE: 70

HOW TO DRINK: Use in cooking, especially recipes calling for vanilla.

MUDDY RIVER DISTILLERY, SPICED CAROLINA RUM,

40% ABV, NORTH CAROLINA, UNITED STATES

AROMA: Vanilla, coffee, and cola

PALATE: Texturally, it feels like a sugared rum not labeled "flavored." Thus, the base's natural state of molasses cookie, cinnamon, and cola come through, but a powerful spice breaks toward the end for a delicious tingle. The finish feels a little sweet. But frankly, if not for the spice and sweetness toward the end, some might be fooled into not recognizing this as a flavored rum.

SCORE: 72

HOW TO DRINK: This is a worthy addition to any spiced rum collector's sipping roster.

OLD MAN GUAVABERRY BRAND, THE ORIGINAL WILD GUAVABERRY ISLAND FOLK LIQUEUR,

35% ABV, SINT MAARTEN

AROMA: Crushed guavaberries, peppers, and cherry

PALATE: Tangy with hints of vanilla, berries, and spice

SCORE: 89

HOW TO DRINK: This is an amazing after-dinner digestive.

PETITE SHRUBB ORANGE LIQUEUR,
35% ABV, MARTINIQUE

AROMA: If heaven had a nose, this is it for an orange lover. It's layered in citrus: lemon, lime, orange, zest, and peel. And mango, coconut, and berries. There are hints of oak, leather, and pepper too.

PALATE: Beautiful. Pure. It feels perfect on the tongue. Not too sweet. Not too tart. Just layered in complex citrus notes, spice, and lovely raw-and-edgy sugarcane. This can and should be enjoyed neat, and as a replacement for all cocktails calling for orange liqueurs.

SCORE: 95

HOW TO DRINK: This could replace half the liqueurs used in creative craft cocktails. If you bartend, find this and mix.

PLANTATION STIGGINS' FANCY PINEAPPLE,
40% ABV, BOTTLED IN FRANCE

AROMA: When pineapple is in the name, it's no surprise that pineapple is on the nose, with hints of mango and peach.

PALATE: Many flavored products are laden with chemicals and do not offer any real artisanship. Not this. It's sublime neat with tangy and sweet hints of fruit, caramel, and vanilla, with a medium nutty finish.

SCORE: 86

HOW TO DRINK: In the hands of a good bartender, Plantation Pineapple creates magic in a glass.

RHUM BARBANCOURT PANGO RHUM,
35% ABV, HAITI

AROMA: Pineapple, grapefruit, orange, lemon, and a hint of coconut

PALATE: Absolutely gorgeous for the citrus lover. Grapefruit is strong—so is the pineapple—but the rum comes through, with hints of molasses and cola.

SCORE: 88

HOW TO DRINK: Highly recommended for cocktails to complement rum in a boozy concoction. Heck, why not try 2 ounces Rhum Barbancourt and 1 ounce Pango stirred, poured over ice, and garnished with a lemon twist?

RON MIEL GUANCHE, HONEY ADDED,
20% ABV, CANARY ISLANDS

AROMA: Sharp cola, vanilla, honey, molasses, and rhubarb

PALATE: Raw honey, as well as processed honey and Honey Nut Cheerios.
The texture is like a thin milkshake. And the honey masks most other
notes until the very end, when blueberry, blackberry, and cherry appear.
But at no point is the rum's essence detected. Nonetheless, if you love
honey, this is a home run.

SCORE: 80

HOW TO DRINK: For cocktails calling for honey, this makes a decent alcohol-
forward replacement.

Despite having an obvious honey note, Ron Miel Guanda offers a hint of blackberry.

RUM-BAR RUM CREAM, WORTHY ESTATE,
15% ABV, WORTHY ESTATE, JAMAICA

AROMA: Condensed milk, tres leches cake, and cream

PALATE: For a cream, you expect this to be milky in texture: this is in the form of a condensed milk with tastes of simple syrup, molasses, and a subtle caramel. It's a sweet bomb over cream.

SCORE: 76

HOW TO DRINK: Add to coffee.

RUMSON'S COFFEE RUM,
40% ABV, BOTTLED IN THE UNITED STATES

AROMA: Well, they certainly used coffee here. This is straight out of a barista's haven, with raw and roasted coffee. After the coffee comes a faint hint of rum.

PALATE: This is just delicious. You wouldn't think a coffee-flavored rum would pack some oak, cigar box, and chocolate, but it does—just before nuts, bold dark-roasted coffee, and cherry cola. The texture is slightly syrupy, but there's a decent finish here, with a hint of cinnamon coffee.

SCORE: 82

HOW TO DRINK: Add to drinks calling for coffee.

SQUEAL SPICED BLACK RUM GO PIG,
45% ABV, COLORADO, UNITED STATES

AROMA: Heavy food coloring, coffee, and molasses, with a slight hint of cardamom

PALATE: The palate is not too dissimilar to a few dark rums, and a few less conscientious distilleries may label this as such. As is, there's vanilla, cocoa, molasses, and caramel. But it's still not complex or overly delicious. It works for what it is.

SCORE: 78

HOW TO DRINK: This makes an excellent dark rum floater.

OPPOSITE: *When Topper's Banana Vanilla Cinnamon says it has banana, well, it really does. It's as pronounced as a fresh banana or plantain on a beach.*

TAILDRAGGER COFFEE FLAVORED RUM BATCH 6,

30%T ABV, ILLINOIS, UNITED STATES

AROMA: Coffee, overcooked pecans, and dirt

PALATE: Much lighter than the nose suggests. This is more like cold coffee than a spirit; rum is masked in the coffee. Still, if you love coffee, this is your style.

SCORE: 60

HOW TO DRINK: Sip cold.

TOPPER'S BANANA VANILLA CINNAMON,

20% ABV, SINT MAARTEN

AROMA: Banana

PALATE: If I were to close my eyes and imagine a vanilla, banana, cinnamon ice-cream float, this is it. It doesn't come off as syrupy or sugary; it's actually quite pleasant on the palate and would make a great mixer.

SCORE: 80

HOW TO DRINK: Use in cocktails calling for banana.

TOPPER'S COCONUT, 21% ABV, SINT MAARTEN

AROMA: Coconut suntan lotion with a hint of green apple

PALATE: The coconut is not as chemical as the nose suggested. Rather, it's more like bagged sugared-and-shredded coconut, with hints of chocolate and fruit.

SCORE: 70

HOW TO DRINK: This is a potential replacement for coconut cream in recipes.

A rural rum shop in Barbados. ALAMY STOCK PHOTO

TOPPER'S MOCHA MAMA, 21% ABV, SINT MAARTEN

AROMA: Coffee roasters' den, dark chocolate, and hazelnut

PALATE: This practically tastes just like a Starbucks hazelnut latte. If you're into coffee flavors, you'll be in heaven.

SCORE: 76

HOW TO DRINK: Add to coffee.

TOPPER'S RHUM SPICED,

40% ABV, SINT MAARTEN

AROMA: Oak, banana, roasted nuts, and pineapple

PALATE: First the rum shines, with vanilla, caramel, and cola appearing over a hint of sugarcane juice. Then, the spice hits very subtly. Quite frankly, this tastes a lot like what some people call rum.

SCORE: 85

HOW TO DRINK: Just sip it if you love spiced rum.

TOPPER'S WHITE CHOCOLATE RASPBERRY,

21% ABV, SINT MAARTEN

AROMA: Melting chocolate, burnt sugar, and plastic

PALATE: Saturated with sweet, syrupy in texture, with hints of raspberry and white chocolate

SCORE: 45

HOW TO DRINK: Not recommended

WICKED DOLPHIN COCONUT RESERVE,

30% ABV, FLORIDA, UNITED STATES

AROMA: Coconut suntan lotion

PALATE: Powdered-sugared coconut

SCORE: 70

HOW TO DRINK: If you like coconut and sugar, sip it.

WICKED DOLPHIN SPICED RESERVE,

40% ABV, FLORIDA, UNITED STATES

AROMA: Clove, cinnamon bark, and vanilla cola

PALATE: Spicy with vanilla and cinnamon

SCORE: 60

HOW TO DRINK: If you're a spiced rum lover, you'll like this in your cabinet.

CHAPTER 7

OTHER CANE SPIRITS

BECAUSE THESE CANE SPIRITS ARE LABELED CATEGORIES OTHER THAN RUM, they deserve their own unique look. Although there are not many in this book, cachaça and arrack are pleasurable tastes and deserve your attention.

AVUÁ CACHAÇA AMBURANA,
40% ABV, CARMO, RIO DE JANEIRO, BRAZIL
AROMA: Grass, alfalfa, oregano, and funk
PALATE: Wood, herbs, spice, and vegetal notes
SCORE: 80
HOW TO DRINK: Quite interesting as a sipper, but this cachaça calls for cocktails to be built around it. Taste and mix!

AVUÁ CACHAÇA OAK,
40% ABV, CARMO, RIO DE JANEIRO, BRAZIL
AROMA: Vegetables, cane juice, oak, and earth
PALATE: What it lacks in aroma it makes up for in palate, but this is leaps and bounds different than your typical Caribbean rum—as all cachaças are. It's earthy, gritty, and raw, from the initial corn grits with a pat of melted butter to the raw molasses cookie dough. Then, hints of tobacco, cherry, and a touch of caramel. Finishes slightly bitter and short, but would make a great cocktail.
SCORE: 79
HOW TO DRINK: Cachaça cocktails

FOLLOWING SPREAD: *Cachaça is a unique product of Brazil and cannot be made anywhere else.* SHUTTERSTOCK

BY THE DUTCH BATAVIA ARRACK,

48% ABV, INDONESIA

AROMA: Fruit, anise, oak, eucalyptus, and earth

PALATE: Very herbal with spice, citrus, black licorice, mushroom, and allspice

SCORE: 82

HOW TO DRINK: Hemingway Daiquiri

CUCA FRESCA CACHAÇA

4-YEAR-OLD, 40% ABV, MINAS GERAIS, BRAZIL

AROMA: Really raw. Think sugarcane cut and pressed with an earthiness, and a yeast note with hints of pepper and sulfur.

PALATE: Much like the nose, it's very raw, ripe with earth and cane, with a handful of baking spices, especially cinnamon.
If you appreciate the base spirit flavor of agricole and cachaça, this is a fun and raw flavor.

SCORE: 82

HOW TO DRINK: Caipirinha

CUCA FRESCA PRATA CACHAÇA,

40% ABV, MINAS GERAIS, BRAZIL

AROMA: Raw cane juice, boiling bamboo shoots

PALATE: Exotic, raw and rich sugarcane, with pepper and green apple

SCORE: 80

HOW TO DRINK: Here's the thing with Cuca Prata: you'll find an overwhelming flavor, but you must like sugarcane. If you do, it's a sipper. Nonetheless, it's a great cocktail base, especially in a Caipirinha or a Bloody Mary.

NOVO FOGO
SINGLE-BARREL 33
3-YEAR-OLD,
44.5% ABV, BRAZIL

AROMA: Passion fruit, grapefruit, pepper, vanilla, floral, and pear

PALATE: Whoa. So many layered fruits dominating the palate, but it's light. Blueberry, mandarin orange, green apple, dried apricot, and cigar. Lovely finish with a touch of cinnamon.

SCORE: 90

HOW TO DRINK: Sip.

Novo Fogo Cachaças lends itself to sipping neat or to simply making mojitos. If you love the taste of sugarcane, you'll love these in mojitos.

NOVO FOGO
SINGLE-BARREL 137
7-YEAR-OLD,
42% ABV, BRAZIL

AROMA: Citrus, floral, honey, oak, cedar, sugarcane, delicate spice, and hints of alfalfa and banana

PALATE: Complex, layered in citrus, marzipan, green apple, pear, watermelon Jolly Rancher, and cinnamon. This is so rich and intense on the palate and tastes so unlike anything else in this book that the flavor is just a beautiful and wild ride. It finishes long and slightly bitter with a hint of oak.

SCORE: 96

HOW TO DRINK: Sip neat. If you add ice, this author will find you. If you use in a cocktail, the Brazilians will find you.

OPPOSITE: *Cuca Fresca Cachaça is partially owned by rapper Snoop Dogg.*

NOVO FOGO SINGLE-BARREL 152 3-YEAR-OLD,

40% ABV, BRAZIL

AROMA: Ripe and fresh sugarcane juice, coconut, fresh-cut grass, petrol, and herbs

PALATE: Oak, spice, nuts, coconut, and a hint of dried fruit. Staunch pepper comes through toward the finish for a delicious and rounded completion.

SCORE: 85

HOW TO DRINK: Sip neat. Those who love spice will fall in love.

NOVO FOGO SINGLE-BARREL 216 2-YEAR-OLD,

45% ABV, BRAZIL

AROMA: Popped corn, oak, marzipan, sugarcane juice, and citrus

PALATE: Very clean and elegant, crisp with oak dryness and hints of almond, walnut shell, and slightly overbaked pie crust

SCORE: 82

HOW TO DRINK: Mojito

CHAPTER 8

COCKTAILS

TIMES SQUARE IS BUSTLING WITH TOURISTS AND PANHANDLERS. Show-goers hustle to their theaters and the taxis honk—because it's New York, where silence is hard to come by and everybody is going somewhere. Tucked away at 228 West 47th Street, attached to the historic Hotel Edison, the Rum House, with its

Making cocktails at home requires a few important instruments: tin shaker, bar spoon, a strainer or two, and a plethora of cocktail glasses. You'll want mixing agents (like Luxardo, for instance) too.

wood-paneled and leatherback decor and candlelit feel, serves as part haven, part rum oasis with an original menu to match the highly skilled bartender's classic mixing skills. And there's some glitz too: the *Birdman* scene where Michael Keaton confronts the play critic was filmed here.

The Rum House, a thriving and profitable bar, hums with cocktail shakers clicking and clacking, corks popping, and the sloshing sound of liquid hitting ice—that's the rum flowing. Most rum bars feel like this, lacking arrogance or pretension, places where any social status feels comfortable to sit down and take a pull of rum. That's the welcoming rum way.

From Smuggler's Cove in San Francisco to the Rum Line in Miami, rum bars—often specialty spots called tiki bars—are pleasure islands with beach shirts, leis, fruit, and laughter. Bartenders rock out, often to no music, as they juice limes, shake daiquiris, and garnish with lemon twists. You might even see a one-armed air drum solo to Journey's "Don't Stop Believin'" as a beach-shirt-wearing bartender pushes the ladder to the back bar, or hear a head-banging offering to Metallica's "Enter Sandman." Rum-centric bartenders have such a good time, they mask the fact that rum takes genuine skill to mix.

It's not like vodka, which is so neutral you can mix with any juice and taste mostly the juice. (If the rum tastes like vodka, you should question if it's really rum.) And rum's not like whiskey, a beautiful spirit but one that has limitations when mixing. It's not like agave-based spirits, where the palate often craves salt. Rich rums could dominate all cocktail recipes single-handedly. But because there are so many options, so many styles, so many rum classics, so many new tiki drinks, bartenders must understand the nuance of each rum.

If a cocktail recipe calls for rum . . . what kind of rum? The agricoles offer vegetal, herbal, and spice nuances that could be unappealing to sweet-tooths, while molasses-based dry rums can be perfect replacements in whiskey drinks. And of course, if you've read this far, you know there's sugar added to many rums, which can throw off a recipe. For the Rum House owner and veteran bartender Kenneth McCoy, his method of choosing rum for mixing starts with a simple taste.

McCoy first finds a flavor he wants to stand out in a cocktail and constructs around that particular ingredient. For example, the London Town cocktail at the Rum House contains Brugal Añejo, pear, and port. But it wasn't the rum that motivated this drink, it was the port—an underused ingredient in modern cocktails. After the flavor decision, he then decides if he wants the drink shaken or stirred.

OPPOSITE: *If you plan to make rum cocktails, you'll need a lot of citrus and mint.*

Generally, though, bartenders build around the base, which in this case is rum. Veteran rum bartender Kate Perry, the general manager at Seattle's Rumba, analyzes rum as sommeliers do wine, because its region, production style, and raw material have so much to do with the final product. "A Cabernet Sauvignon from California and from France are similar on paper, but showcase wildly different experiences. The same goes for rum, if you put a Jamaican and a Puerto Rican rum side-by-side you might think you have two very different spirits, and really, you do," Perry says. "I like to make 'whiskey-style' cocktails like your Old Fashioneds and Manhattans with very dry, lean, well-aged rums. Appleton 12 Year and Brugal Extra Viejo are two of my favorites. For exotic, tropical drinks, a blend of Guyana (for the richness) and Jamaican (for the funk) works best. Classic Cuban drinks like Daiquiris and Mojitos require a lean, light bodied rum."

The daiquiri seems to be the bartender's cocktail lynchpin, but few agree on what rum makes the best daiquiri. Some like lighter rums, as Perry said, and others want younger blends to allow the nuance from a pot still to shine through. "A younger rum, like a Mount Gay Black Barrel (a blend), in a daiquiri really comes through. You get the vanilla but don't lose the characteristics. I'm also a big fan of Plantation," says Max Solano, the former head mixologist for celebrity chef Emeril Lagasse's restaurants.

Few people agree on which rum makes the best cocktail. SHUTTERSTOCK

Solano's methods are more common than McCoy's, who prefers dark rums. "I use two ounces of Appleton Estate, three quarters simple syrup, and three quarter of lime juice. To me, that makes the perfect-tasting daiquiri. You've sort of just got a complete right down the middle, not too sweet, not too sour, with your citrus," McCoy says.

When he orders a daiquiri, *Esquire* food critic John Mariani gives the bartender his card, with the recipe on the back. It calls for gold rum. In a sense, the daiquiri's rum is as much preference as anything, but the methods are not. If a bartender interview candidate can't make a daiquiri or automatically throws ingredients into the blender, he or she will not be hired at any serious bar, let alone at a rum bar.

As for having the right rum for the right cocktail, the strategies vary, and most bartenders are flexible enough to roll with the trends and to meet a customer's desires. And the wide range of styles gives rum unlimited mixing possibilities. Solano says the diversity of proofs and countries provide an incredible flavor-profile range. "Rum is the best-value brown-spirits category," he says.

In contrast to the sipping consumer advocates who are against sweeteners, bartenders largely don't mind the use of additives. "If you think about it, the base ingredient of rum is from sugarcane. Yes, they're adding sugar, but if you're adding acidity in cocktail, you offset that. It's about flavor," Solano says. "Are you still getting cane, molasses, and barrel extraction?"

While sugar doesn't bother her, Perry does treat additive rum differently than unadulterated cane spirits. "I save the sweet stuff for after-dinner drinks: a night cap of El Dorado 12 Year or Plantation 20th Anniversary is a beautiful thing on its own," she says.

Of course, a sugar-added rum does influence a bartender's ingredients. "If I was using a rum that was sweet, I would not be adding a lot of sugar, because if it's got a sweetness to it already, you don't need a lot," McCoy says.

On the other end of the spectrum, many professional bartenders prefer the rawness of agricole and other cane-based spirits, such as cachaça, "which has a strong note of sweet banana chips, spiced rums which use cloves, cinnamon, and vanilla to name a few," says Cody Goldstein, an East Coast cocktail consultant. "It's a beautiful style of cane spirit with maturity. Anything I would make rum cocktails with, I'd use cachaça. Some have pronounced baking spice and cinnamon."

Solano agrees but says cachaça is underutilized.

In fact, agricoles and cachaça make great replacements in whiskey cocktails, Solano says. Think Old Fashioneds, where you're adding sugar, bitters, and water, or a Manhattan, where you're mixing with vermouth. "You can sub out the base spirit of whiskey for cachaça if you're looking for the essence of sugarcane. Cachaça captures more of the cane characteristic than most rum. A lot of rums get lost in whiskey-substitute cocktails."

On that note, Perry has made a career out of making sure agricoles and cachaça do not get lost in cocktails or forgotten behind the bar. But she admits that home bartenders may struggle with the complexity and grassy and vegetal nature of these spirits:

> Using Rhum Agricole at home can be a challenge, for sure. I think that it's the same as a first experience with coffee: new consumers tend to put lots of cream and sugar into their drink until they get a taste for its nature. Then they tend to back off the cushion, and more adventurous palates tend to seek out stronger, unsweetened coffee and perhaps the funky Ethiopian bean. The same is true about wine: first sippers enjoy accessible Cabernets and lush Syrahs, but the more one's palate is accustomed to the flavor, the more one enjoys the more flavorful drink. Same is true with r(h)um: the Zacapa, Diplomático Exclusiva, Zayas of the world are the gateway—and the funky Jamaican and French-style agricole are the horizon.
>
> In terms of mixing, I always advise simple at first. Make simple cocktails well. Make an unaged agricole or cachaça as a Daiquiri. Try an aged agricole or cachaça as an Old Fashioned. Find the things that you enjoy and then build on that. The sugar and bitters or lime will soften the edges of the spirit and make probably the most complex, simple drink you have tried. Really dig an unaged rhum Daiquiri? Try subbing out the simple syrup for pineapple or nutmeg syrup. Super into that zebrawood-finished Cachaça Old Fashioned? Mix up your bitters: try chocolate mole or cardamom bitters instead. Find your base level of enjoyment and add other flavors that you love! There is no right answer in cocktail-making, as every palate is unique. Find what you love and run with it.

Fortunately for today's drinker, yesterday's bartenders loved mixing with rum and created such rum classics as the daiquiri, Hemingway Daiquiri, Hurricane, mai tai, piña colada, original rum punch, mojito, El Presidente, and Dark 'N Stormy. There's also a great selection of new cocktails that are easy to make at home.

Pairing Food with Rum

Perhaps rum's greatest weakness—pairing with food—could be its greatest strength. The problem is that not enough restaurants carry the rum arsenal one needs to properly make pairings. But when they do, watch out!

Seattle's Rumba has both the collection and talent to properly pair rum with food. The trick, says Kate Perry, veteran rum bartender and Rumba's general manager, is to look for food that brings out the different characteristics in the spirit—a different strategy than with wine, where sommeliers try to complement the food.

"The range of rum is so fascinating that a bowl of cashews with a light bodied rum, a funky Jamaican, and something rich from Colombia would all give you very different experiences," Perry says. "Sometimes you might want to complement your delicious morsel with a rum that is completely opposite in flavor, and sometimes you might want to match richness with richness, leanness with leanness. We serve a coconut battered bananas foster with coconut ice cream and buttered rum sauce at the bar that is absolutely divine with the likes of Ron Zacapa or other notably rich rums."

The rum cocktail can offer complexity similar to that of wine. The acidity in many drinks can cut fat on the palate, and the mellowness of a good punch may deliver the complexity one looks for with lighter proteins, such as a fillet or roasted chicken. "A classic punch tends to be mellow in character and easy to drink, pairing naturally with food," Perry says. "The fun thing about punch is that it can also be whatever you decide, and you could tailor it to the evening's menu. . . . Punch would be the optimal rum cocktail pair."

Pairing cocktails is one thing, but pairing rum neat is another. If you love the taste of spirit, rum goes great with fried foods, meats, stews, pies, and heavy fish.

El Presidente

1½ oz.	rich unaged rum (*Rum Curious* choice: Cartavio Silver)
1½ oz.	Dolin Vermouth Blanc (Martini & Rossi or Cinzano Bianco are fine substitutes)
1	bar spoon Orange Curaçao or Grand Marnier
½	bar spoon real grenadine
1	thinly cut orange peel

TOOLS: Bar spoon, mixing glass, strainer

GARNISH: Maraschino cherry (optional)

GLASSWARE: Cocktail

METHOD: Stir ingredients with ice and strain into a chilled glass. Add the thin orange peel and cherry.

Life's a Beach by Jim Romdall

1½ oz.	Novo Fogo Silver Cachaça
1½ oz.	Lustau Fino Sherry
¾ oz.	lime juice
2 oz.	watermelon juice
2 oz.	Bundaberg Ginger Beer

METHOD: Build all in tall glass and add ice, garnish with an umbrella, and pretend you're on a beach!

Classic Daiquiri

Americans abuse the daiquiri with blenders and ice. Created by an American iron miner in Cuba, the original daiquiri recipe includes six lemons, 6 tablespoons of sugar, 1.4 ounces of Bacardi rum, and ½ ounce of mineral water with crushed ice. But this recipe has been altered into what is now known as the Classic Daiquiri.

2 oz.	rum
1 oz.	fresh lime juice
½ oz.	simple syrup

METHOD: Combine in a shaker with ice, shake vigorously, and strain into a chilled glass.

The daiquiri is as classic and simple as they come. This tasty concoction is the de facto interview for all bartenders. If you can't make a classic daiquiri, your bartending skills are suspect.

Dark 'N Stormy

This cocktail's roots begin in Bermuda with 1800s-era sailors mixing local rum with ginger. But the contemporary story is much more interesting. The rum company Gosling's Brothers, which was the first known rum used in this cocktail, trademarked the name Dark 'N Stormy as well as other rum-related cocktails. Goslings sued Pernod Ricard for using "Black Stormy," claiming it infringed upon its trademark. It also sent a cease-and-desist letter to the blog InuAKena.com for asking readers: "What's the best rum for a Dark and Stormy?"

2 oz.	Gosling's dark rum
	chilled ginger beer
	lime wedge

GLASSWARE: Highball
METHOD: Fill a highball glass with ice, add rum and ginger beer, squeeze lime, and stir. Drink. And don't forget Gosling's or use their trademark if you're sending emails.

Painkiller

Pusser's owns this trademark, so most, not all, "published" recipes use Pusser's. It was created in the 1970s in the British Virgin Islands at a bar called Soggy Dollar Bar.

2 oz.	Pusser's rum
4 oz.	pineapple juice
½ oz.	cream of coconut
½ oz.	orange juice

GARNISH: Sprinkle of nutmeg
METHOD: Mix together, shake, and garnish.

Hemingway Daiquiri

It probably doesn't take you long to figure out this cocktail was named after booze-loving and brilliant author Ernest Hemingway, who once said, "I drink to make other people more interesting." While in Cuba, Hemingway drank a cocktail called the El Papa Doble, which consisted of 3¾ ounces of Bacardi, two limes, half a grapefruit, and six drops of maraschino, mixed in an electric mixer, and served over shaved ice. The Hemingway Daiquiri was created in his honor and with a little less booze.

2 oz.	unaged rum
¾ oz.	fresh grapefruit juice
½ oz.	lime juice
¼ oz.	Luxardo Maraschino Liqueur
¼ oz.	simple syrup

GARNISH: Grapefruit

METHOD: Shake all ingredients and serve with a grapefruit twist.

Ernest Hemingway loved to drink, and this is his grapefruit-forward self in drink form.

London Town by Kenneth McCoy

2 oz.	Brugal Añejo rum
½ oz.	tawny port
½ oz.	Rothman & Winter Orchard Pear Liqueur

GARNISH: Lemon peel or twist

GLASSWARE: Coupe

METHOD: Combine all ingredients in a mixing glass. Add ice and stir for 30 seconds, then strain into a chilled coupe. Garnish with a lemon peel or twist.

The London Town by Kenneth McCoy. PAUL WAGTOUICZ

Piña Colada

Of all the rum drinks, the piña colada seems to be enshrined in the musician hall of fame. Rupert Holmes's "Escape (The Piña Colada Song)" captures the hearts of beach-shirt wearers everywhere, but the cocktail is also in the lyrics of songs by Garth Brooks, Steely Dan, Lonestar, Patrick Sébastien, the Grateful Dead, and many others. According to the *Pittsburgh Press*'s 1928 column "Wherein a City Takes on a Leer" by Florence Fisher Parry, who became a bestselling children's writer, the piña colada was a "famous Cuban drink, albeit a soft drink, made of pure pineapple juice so vigorously frapped in ice that it became smooth and opaque, resembling rich milk with a high collar on it, delicious to the thirst." Parry's piña colada mention corroborates Cuban confectioner texts that suggested this early piña colada was rum free. However, her writing vaguely alluded to Bacardi being mixed with fruit, slightly opening the door of possibility that rum was mixed when she discovered this drink "Twelve years ago when I was in Havana." The Piña Colada's creation has never been clear, but the Puerto Rican Hilton claims it created the modern recipe in 1954, even though recipes were published in the 1940s and 1950s. A 1944 *Pittsburgh Post-Gazette* article offered a crude Piña Colada recipe: combine coconut and pineapple. "For something really different, try adding ice cream . . . the outcome will be a refreshing frosted drink. Then, too, you can add rum for a grand rum cocktail." Whoever created this cocktail probably should have bought shares in a blender company.

2 oz.	rum
½ oz.	lime juice
1 oz.	pineapple juice
1 oz.	cream of coconut
1 oz.	coconut milk
1 cup	ice (or vanilla ice cream)

GARNISH: Pineapple wedge

GLASSWARE: Hurricane

METHOD: Add ingredients to a blender, blend to your smoothness satisfaction, and pour into a hurricane glass. Garnish with a pineapple wedge and don't forget the umbrella.

Mai Tai

The mai tai's origins cannot really be disputed. Its creator, Victor J. "Trader Vic" Bergeron, penned an essay in 1970 discussing the reasons for the drink and its evolution. He wrote, "In 1944, after success with several exotic rum drinks, I felt a new drink was needed . . . I was at the service bar in my Oakland restaurant. I took down a bottle of 17-year-old rum. It was J. Wray Nephew from Jamaica; surprisingly golden in color, medium-bodied, but with the rich pungent flavor particular to the Jamaican blends. The flavor of this great rum wasn't meant to be overpowered with heavy additions of fruit juices and flavorings. I took a fresh lime, added some orange curaçao from Holland, a dash of Rock Candy Syrup, and a dollop of French Orgeat, for its subtle almond flavor. A generous amount of shaved ice and vigorous shaking by hand produced the marriage I was after. Half the lime shell went in for color . . . I stuck in a branch of fresh mint and gave two of them to Ham and Carrie Guild, friends from Tahiti, who were there that night. Carrie took one sip and said, 'Mai Tai—Roa Ae.' In Tahitian this means 'Out of This World—The Best.' Well, that was that. I named the drink 'Mai Tai.'" The mai tai would see many variations, and Bergeron became famous for the drink, creating his own line of products and practically making orgeat syrup a mainstay in bars.

2 oz.	Jamaican rum (*Rum Curious* choice: Appleton 12)
½ oz.	orgeat
½ oz.	Holland DeKuyper Orange Curaçao
¼ oz.	Rock Candy Syrup
	juice from 1 fresh lime

GARNISH: Mint

METHOD: Vigorously shake ingredients with half a lime in a shaker, pour over ice, and garnish with mint.

OPPOSITE: *The mai tai was a hotly debated cocktail until its creator penned an essay in the 1970s. Since then, the drink has been all over the place, and now people call for the creator's name, a Trader Vic Mai Tai.*

The Hurricane

2 oz.	light rum
2 oz.	dark rum
2 oz.	passion fruit juice
1 oz.	orange juice
½ oz.	fresh lime juice
1	tablespoon simple syrup
1	tablespoon grenadine

GARNISH: Orange slice and cherry

GLASSWARE: Hurricane

METHOD: Shake all ingredients in a cocktail shaker with ice, then strain into a hurricane glass filled with ice. Garnish with a cherry and orange slice.

ABOVE: *A worker at the Neisson distillery in Martinique.* GETTY IMAGES
OPPOSITE: *Nothing says rum fun like a tiki mug. These beautiful mugs are widely available, and if you don't have one, don't worry—you can still sip the Fool's Gold in a solo cup or rocks glass. But will it taste the same?*

PRO-LEVEL RUM COCKTAIL RECIPES BY MAX A. SOLANO

These high-level rum cocktails are for the advanced home bartenders or the pros working behind the bar. Of course, if you can read directions, you can make them too. I chose Max Solano for these recipes because he's made some of the best rum drinks I've ever tasted. This may sound odd, since he's considered a whiskey guy, but Solano understands the intricacies of rum from a tasting perspective and knows how to bring balance to each style. As well as being former head mixologist for Emeril Lagasse's restaurants, Solano was winner of the 2016 Wholesaler Iron Mixologist Competition and is now the primary mixologist for Southern Wine & Spirits of Nevada.

Modernista Colada

2 oz.	house-made spice-infused Botran Reserva rum*
1 oz.	Wilks & Wilson pineapple gomme syrup
1 oz.	fresh lemon juice
1 oz.	cream of coconut (Calahua, Coco Lopez, etc.)

TOPPING: Mocha-espresso foam**

GARNISH: Two candied pineapple chunks on a skewer, sprinkle of ground cinnamon

GLASSWARE: Highball

METHOD: In a mixing glass or tin, combine all of the ingredients except for the foam and shake well over ice. Strain the contents into a highball glass over fresh ice. Top off with the foam and garnish.

* For each 750-milliliter bottle of Botran Reserva rum, incorporate 4 ounces sliced fresh ginger root, 4 cinnamon sticks (cracked), 4 whole nutmegs (cracked), 2 tablespoons whole cloves (cracked), 2 tablespoons whole allspice (cracked), and 2 whole Madagascar vanilla beans (stripped). Keep the infusion resting for 3 to 5 days, agitating its contents once a day. Once the infusion is complete, strain the rum through cheesecloth until there's no remaining sediment.

** Take a clean whipped-cream siphon (1 US quart) and place into it the following: 4 ounces egg whites (pasteurized preferable), 10 ounces espresso coffee, 5 ounces Godiva Dark Chocolate Liqueur, and 1 ounce fresh lemon juice. Twist the top and shake well. Before placing the N20 cartridge, taste the mix and make sure it's neither too bitter nor too sweet—tweak where applicable. Add the first cartridge and shake well for 10 seconds. Discard the cartridge and insert the second. Again, shake well for 10 to 15 seconds. Foam should be ready to test—be gentle when pulling on the handle. For better results, place in a cooler or refrigerator upside down for 24 hours to allow better stabilization. And always shake if laid to rest before using again.

Caution: *Do not* twist open the canister while there's still gas inside.

Golden Age

2 oz.	El Dorado 15-Year-Old rum
¼ oz.	Luxardo Maraschino Liqueur
¼ oz.	brown sugar–cinnamon syrup*
3 dashes	The Bitter Truth Grapefruit Bitters
2 dashes	Fee Brothers Old Fashion Aromatic Bitters
2	grapefruit swaths

GARNISH: Grapefruit peel, Luxardo cherry flag on skewer

GLASSWARE: Double old-fashioned

METHOD: Place the grapefruit peel, syrup, and bitters in a mixing glass or beaker and muddle well. Add the rum, liqueur, and ice and stir well (35 to 40 rotations).

Strain the contents into a double old-fashioned glass over a large ice sphere or block. Garnish.

* Make a brown sugar syrup by using equal parts granulated brown sugar and hot water. Combine both and stir well until the sugar is fully dissolved. While still warm, add 10 to 12 cracked cinnamon sticks and infuse for up to 3 days. Filter out all of the sediment by using a cheesecloth.

Vinho Carousel

1½ oz.	Dos Maderas 5+3 rum
1 oz.	Sandeman Tawny Porto
1½ oz.	Funkin Passion Fruit Purée
¾ oz.	Fee Brothers Orgeat Syrup
¾ oz.	pasteurized egg whites
6–7 dashes	The Bitter Truth Jerry Thomas' Own Decanter Bitters

GARNISH: Orange rectangle peel and Luxardo cherry flag on metal pick

GLASSWARE: Coupe

METHOD: In a mixing glass or tin, combine all of the ingredients and dry shake well. Add ice and shake well once more. Strain the contents straight up into a chilled coupe glass. Garnish.

Shrunken Head

1½ oz.	Gosling's Black Seal rum
¾ oz.	Kai coconut water
½ oz.	The Bitter Truth Pimento Dram
1½ oz.	cream of coconut (Calahua, Coco Lopez, etc.)
1 oz.	fresh lime juice
¼ oz.	homemade cinnamon-maple syrup*
	homemade pineapple whipped cream

GARNISH: Toasted coconut, two fire sticks, one edible flower

GLASSWARE: Fresh brown coconut

METHOD: In a mixing glass or tin, combine all of the ingredients except for the pineapple whipped cream and shake well over ice. Strain the contents into a hollowed-out fresh brown coconut over crushed or pebble ice. Top it off with the whipped cream and garnish.

* For every 8 ounces grade A 100 percent maple syrup, add 2 tablespoons of ground cinnamon. Place the contents into a blender and frappe for 8 to 10 seconds. Empty the contents into a narrow container and let sit for 10 to 12 hours. Scoop out the top layer of compiled cinnamon and filter the rest through cloth until most of the sediment is gone. Note: Not all of the cinnamon grounds will be removed. Always shake before use. Keeping syrup refrigerated will make it last for months.

Sassy Sandía

1½ oz.	Ron Atlantico Blanco
¾ oz.	Joseph Cartron Ginger Liqueur
3 oz.	cold-pressed watermelon juice
1½ oz.	fresh lime sour (1:1 ratio fresh lime juice to simple syrup)
1 pinch	pink sea salt
2 oz.	Fever-Tree Ginger Beer

GARNISH: Thin watermelon triangle crisp, fresh mint sprig

GLASSWARE: Collins

METHOD: In a mixing glass or tin, combine all of the ingredients except for the ginger beer and shake well over ice. Strain the contents into the Collins glass over 1-inch ice cubes. Add the ginger beer and lightly stir. Garnish.

Sand Dollar

1½ oz.	Mount Gay Black Barrel rum
¾ oz.	St. Germain
1 oz.	fresh lemon juice
¾ oz.	Fee Brothers Orgeat Syrup
3 dashes	Bitter Truth Lemon Bitters

GARNISH: Lavender sugar rim*, dehydrated lemon wheel (and lemon zest)

GLASSWARE: Coupe

METHOD: Rim a chilled coupe glass with lavender sugar and set aside. In a mixing glass or tin, combine all of the ingredients and shake well over ice. Strain the contents straight up into the chilled coupe glass. Garnish.

* Crush dried lavender well, until powdered. Use 2 parts granulated sugar to the crushed lavender and mix well.

For Rum Sakes

1½ oz.	Diplomático Añejo
½ oz.	Boissiere Dry Vermouth
1 oz.	fresh lemon juice
¾ oz.	homemade honey-ginger syrup*
3–4 dashes	The Bitter Truth Grapefruit Bitters

GARNISH: Candied ginger slice, Luxardo cherry flag

GLASSWARE: Coupe

METHOD: In a mixing glass or tin, combine all of the ingredients and shake well over ice. Strain the contents straight up into the chilled coupe glass. Garnish.

* For quickest results, use equal parts clover honey and a premade ginger syrup, such as Wilks & Wilson or homemade, and mix well together so it's no longer separated. It will be ready to use right away.

The Golden Swizzle

1 oz.	El Dorado 8-Year-Old
1 oz.	Yellow Chartreuse
1 oz.	fresh lemon juice
¾ oz.	Wilks & Wilson Penelope's Pineapple Gomme Syrup
2 dashes	Fee Brothers Whiskey Barrel-Aged Bitters

GARNISH: Thin pineapple slice, fresh mint sprig, sugarcane swizzle

GLASSWARE: Zombie

METHOD: In a zombie glass, build the cocktail by adding each of the ingredients. Add crushed or pebble ice and use a swizzle stick to mix the drink. Pack it with more ice and garnish.

Island Batida (Bachida)

1½ oz.	Rhum Barbancourt 3 Star rum
1 oz.	Briottet Crème de Banane Liqueur
1½ oz.	pineapple juice
1½ oz.	condensed milk
½ oz.	cinnamon syrup

GARNISH: Fresh pineapple wedge, pineapple leaf, freshly grated nutmeg

GLASSWARE: Highball

METHOD: In a mixing glass or tin, combine all of the ingredients and shake well over ice. Strain the contents into a highball over fresh crushed or pebble ice. Garnish.

OPPOSITE: *The rum swizzle is a Bermuda drink that's essentially lemon, rum, falernum, and orange juice. Many new rum drinks take on the "swizzle" name, such as this Golden Swizzle. And why not? The swizzle sounds right.*

That Cheeky Hemingway!

2 oz.	Havana Club 7-Year-Old rum
1 oz.	fresh lime juice
¾ oz.	brown sugar syrup
1	bar spoon Lucid absinthe (for rinse)

TOPPING: Marasca cherry and tangerine foam*

GARNISH: Grated cinnamon, Luxardo cherry on skewer

GLASSWARE: Coupe

METHOD: Fill a coupe glass with ice and set it aside. In a mixing glass or tin, combine all of the ingredients except for the foam and shake well over ice. Next, discard the ice from the coupe glass and add one bar spoon of the absinthe. Give it a good swirl and rinse it out. Strain the contents from the shaker straight up into the coupe glass. Top off with the foam and garnish.

* Take a clean whipped-cream siphon (1 US quart) and place in it the following: 5 ounces egg whites (pasteurized preferable), 10 ounces Fruitations tangerine syrup, 4 ounces Luxardo Maraschino Liqueur, and 2 ounces fresh lemon juice. Twist the top and shake well. Before placing the N20 cartridge, taste the mix and make sure it's neither too sour nor too sweet—tweak where applicable. Add the first cartridge and shake well for 10 seconds. Discard the cartridge and insert the second. Again, shake well for 10 to 15 seconds. Foam should be ready to test—be gentle when pulling on the handle. For better results, place in a cooler or refrigerator upside down for 24 hours to allow better stabilization. And always shake if laid to rest before using again.

Caution: *Do not* twist open the canister while there's still gas inside.

The Final Say (Barrel-Aged Concept)*

1 oz.	Gosling's Family Reserve Old Rum
¾ oz.	Yellow Chartreuse
¾ oz.	Luxardo Maraschino
¾ oz.	fresh lemon juice

GARNISH: Dehydrated lemon wheel, lemon zest

GLASSWARE: Coupe

METHOD: In a mixing glass or tin, pour 2½ ounces barrel-aged mix along with ¾ ounce fresh lemon juice. Shake well over ice and strain straight up into a chilled coupe glass. Garnish.

* Recommended aging time is 30 to 45 days in the barrel. Be sure to prep the barrel before its use. Add the rum, Chartreuse, and Luxardo and let it sit. Be sure to filter the contents before using.

Do as the French (Barrel-Aged Concept)*

1½ oz.	Plantation Original Dark rum
¾ oz.	Lejay Crème de Cassis
¾ oz.	Cinzano Bianco Vermouth
¾ oz.	fresh lime juice
3–4 dashes	Australian Bitters

GARNISH: Thin, fresh lime wheel, one spritz orange-flower water (in atomizer)

GLASSWARE: Double old-fashioned

METHOD: In a mixing glass or beaker, combine 3 ounces barrel-aged mix along with ¾ ounce fresh lime juice and stir well over ice. Strain the contents into a double old-fashioned glass over a large ice sphere. Garnish.

* Recommended aging time is 30 to 45 days in the barrel. Be sure to prep the barrel before its use. Add the rum, Crème de Cassis, and vermouth and let it sit. Be sure to filter the contents before using.

Caña Sour

1¾ oz.	Pusser's rum
1 oz.	fresh lemon juice
¾ oz.	Fee Brothers Orgeat Syrup
¾ oz.	Pedro Ximénez sherry (to float)

GARNISH: Thin, fresh lemon wheel, Luxardo cherry flag, fresh mint sprig

GLASSWARE: Double old-fashioned

METHOD: In a mixing glass or tin, combine all of the ingredients except for the sherry and shake well over ice. Strain the contents into a double old-fashioned glass over fresh ice. Float the sherry on top. Garnish.

Leyenda Milk Punch

1½ oz.	Pampero Aniversario rum
1½ oz.	Oloroso sherry
½ oz.	Licor 43
½ oz.	homemade honey syrup*
3 oz.	whole milk

GARNISH: Freshly grated nutmeg, cinnamon stick

GLASSWARE: Collins

METHOD: In a mixing glass or tin, combine all of the ingredients and shake well over ice. Strain the contents into a Collins glass over crushed or pebble ice. Garnish.

* Take equal parts clover honey to warm water and mix well. Refrigerate after use.

Fool's Gold

1½ oz.	Pyrat rum
1 oz.	Wild Turkey 101 Rye
¾ oz.	Marie Brizard Apry Liqueur
¾ oz.	fresh lime juice
¾ oz.	Wilks & Wilson Giovanna's Ginger Syrup
¼ oz.	homemade 5-spiced simple syrup*
½ oz.	Goya Mango Nectar
3 dashes	Australian Bitters

GARNISH: Umbrella, fresh lime wheel, edible flower

GLASSWARE: Tiki mug

METHOD: In a mixing glass or tin, combine all of the ingredients and shake well over ice. Strain the contents into a tiki mug over crushed or pebble ice. Garnish.

* Use Torani Vanilla Bean Syrup as a base. For each 750-milliliter bottle of syrup, incorporate 3 tablespoons of the following: ground cinnamon, ground nutmeg, ground ginger (or ground allspice), and ground clove. Stick all of the ingredients into a blender and frappe for 15 to 20 seconds. Next, pour the contents from the blender into a narrow container and let sit for several hours. Once it's ready, scoop off the cap of spices. The syrup will now undergo several passes through cheesecloth until most of the sediment is collected. Keep refrigerated, and it will last for several weeks.

Alternatively, vacuum sealing for 3 to 4 days after scooping the spice cap will further intensify the spices.

APPENDIX A

Distillery Production Notes

IN THIS SECTION, YOU'LL FIND IMPORTANT PRODUCTION DETAILS that might suggest a brand's flavor profile. For example, if one identifies its source as cane juice, you'll likely detect more raw cane or earthiness. If sugar is added, one can expect sweetness. Or if fresh cane juice is used and at lower distillation points, you'll find more rawness and earth.

These notes were gathered from the distilleries themselves, previously published material, and a few sources within the organizations.

PRECEDING SPREAD: *The foot of Jamaica's Nassau Mountains, very near where Appleton Estate rum is made.* SHUTTERSTOCK

OPPOSITE: *Workers at the Bacardi rum bottling plant circa 1955.* GETTY IMAGES

ABOVE: *Four million gallons of rum arrive at the West India Docks in London, October 10, 1919.* BRIDGEMAN IMAGES

APPLETON ESTATE

LOCATION: Jamaica

WATER SOURCE: Water is from the estate's blazing blue spring that has been filtered by nature as it percolates for miles through the limestone hills of the Cockpit Country before it upwells on the Appleton Estate.

SOURCE MATERIAL: Master blender Joy Spence says, "We grow our own sugarcane on the Appleton Estate. Once the cane is harvested, it is brought to the factory where the cane is washed, chopped, and milled to extract the cane's sweet juice. The juice is then converted into sugar, and the byproduct of this process is molasses, and this is what we use to make our rum."

DISTILLATION: Appleton Estate rum is a blend of pot and column of varying ages. The distillery has five 5,000-gallon pot stills. These pot stills consist of a copper kettle, a

Joy Spence is one of the world's most respected blenders. She works for Appleton Estate.

high wine retort, a low wine retort, and a collector. Says Spence, "The pot distillation method produces a fuller, more flavorful rum than the column-distillation method, and it is the rums produced on these stills that are the heart of every Appleton Estate Jamaica Rum blend and impart to our rums their unique character and the beautiful orange-peel top note, which is a hallmark of the brand. This orange-peel top note is a result of the unique shape of the pot stills, as well as the fact that the pot stills at Appleton Estate are 100 percent copper (rather than copper lined)." In addition, Appleton Estate has triple-column, stainless-steel continuous stills. According to Spence, the stainless steel continuous stills at the Appleton Estate produce a very "clean," light-flavored rum, which is perfect for balancing the robust and flavorful rums produced on their copper pot stills.

OFF-THE-STILL PROOF: For pot still, it is 86% ABV. Column still is 96% ABV.

BARREL-ENTRY PROOF: All rum goes into the barrel at 80% ABV.

COLOR ADDED: Small amounts of caramel for aged rums

SUGAR ADDED: None

BACARDI

LOCATION: Puerto Rico

OFF-THE-STILL PROOF: 77.5% ABV

The cover of a 1934 Bacardi rum brochure produced by Schenley Distillers Corporation. BRIDGEMAN IMAGES

BALCONES RUM

LOCATION: Waco, Texas, United States
WATER SOURCE: Municipal water
DISTILLATION: Pot
OFF-THE-STILL PROOF: 70% ABV
BARREL-ENTRY PROOF: 67.3% ABV

BAYOU PORTFOLIO

LOCATION: Louisiana, United States
WATER SOURCE: Thornwell Aquifer deep well water
SOURCE MATERIAL: Louisiana sugarcane molasses and raw
  Louisiana sugar crystals from Louisiana farms
DISTILLATION: Vendome copper pot stills—one for
  stripping run and one for spirit run
OFF-THE-STILL PROOF: 80% to 82% ABV
BARREL-ENTRY PROOF: 60% ABV
MATURATION: American oak ex-bourbon barrels
FILTRATION: Charcoal
COLOR ADDED: None
SUGAR ADDED: Unknown

Bayou Rum is a rising American star in craft distilling. Located in Louisiana, it stays true to its roots by using only state-grown cane. BAYOU RUM

BLACK CORAL

LOCATION: Riviera Beach, Florida, United States
WATER SOURCE: 5-stage carbon-filtered, UV-sterilized,
  rested water with calcium added
SOURCE MATERIAL: 100 percent Florida blackstrap molasses
OFF-THE-STILL PROOF: 72.5% ABV
BARREL-ENTRY PROOF: 60% ABV
MATURATION: New 36-month air-seasoned white American
  oak, for a minimum of 6 months.
FILTRATION: Coconut-husk carbon
COLOR ADDED: None
SUGAR ADDED: None

BOUKMAN BOTANICAL RHUM

LOCATION: Croix-des-Bouquets and Cap-Haïtien, Haiti

OFF-THE-STILL PROOF: 75% ABV off copper and stainless-steel column still.

FILTRATION: Chill filtered

COLOR ADDED: Nonsweetening caramel

FLAVORING: Boukman is a *clairin trempé*, Haiti's tradition of naturally infused agricole rhums, and uses wood and bark (*liane bandé, zou'devant, campèche, bois cochon*, Limousin oak), bitter-orange peel, allspice, cinnamon ceylonica, clove, natural vanilla extract, and natural bitter almond extract

CHARBAY

LOCATION: Saint Helena, California, United States

WATER SOURCE: Mendocino County well water

SOURCE MATERIAL: Maui and Jamaica sugarcane syrup

OFF-THE-STILL PROOF: 68% ABV

BARREL-ENTRY PROOF: 68% ABV

MATURATION: Stainless steel and French oak.

FILTRATION: None

COLOR ADDED: None

SUGAR ADDED: None

COLD STABILIZATION: None

COCKSPUR

LOCATION: West Indies Distillery, Barbados

WATER SOURCE: Underground water, reverse osmosis

SOURCE MATERIAL: Molasses

DISTILLATION: West Indies has several column stills, but mostly uses one automated column

OFF-THE-STILL PROOF: 95% ABV

BARREL-ENTRY PROOF: 65% ABV

COLOR ADDED: Yes

SUGAR ADDED: None

DEADHEAD

LOCATION: Chiapas, Mexico

SOURCE MATERIAL: Molasses is distilled in the column; cane juice is distilled in the pot.

DISTILLATION: Double-distilled (both pot and column).

OFF-THE-STILL PROOF: 55% ABV pot still, 75% ABV column still

BARREL-ENTRY PROOF: 40% ABV to 45% ABV

MATURATION: 5 to 7 years in American oak (80%) and Chiapas oak wood (20%).

FILTRATION: Charcoal before resting, maturation, and filter press

COLOR ADDED: None

SUGAR ADDED: None

DEPAZ

LOCATION: Saint-Pierre, Martinique

WATER SOURCE: Eau de la Montagne

SOURCE MATERIAL: Cane

OFF-THE-STILL PROOF: Unknown

MATURATION: Blends of 7- to 10-year-old rums

FILTRATION: Filter "à cartouches"

COLOR ADDED: None

SUGAR ADDED: None

OPPOSITE: *A rum-running boat caught by the authorities, twentieth century.* BRIDGEMAN IMAGES

DIPLOMÁTICO PORTFOLIO

LOCATION: Andes Mountains area in La Miel, Venezuela

WATER SOURCE: Five deep wells. Distillery officials said, "These subterranean waters have their origin in the Terepaima National Park. They are pollution free."

SOURCE MATERIAL: The company says its rums are developed from sugarcane honey and molasses. Sugarcane honey comes from the Spanish phrase *miel de cana*, and there is a little lost in translation. Mixologist blog *Elemental Mixology* wrote in 2010, "In the case of 'sugarcane honey,' not only is one set of traditional terms flushed [forms of molasses], another word, 'honey,' begins to be robbed of clear meaning. I think that (in English, at least) the word 'honey' should be reserved for nectar that has been stored by bees." Diplomático's use of "sugarcane honey" is a subject of rum-nerd controversy, to say the least.

OFF-THE-STILL PROOF: From continuous columns, 96.4% ABV; from batch-kettle distillation (this means component fractions are separated before distillation and it's distilled in batches), 96.4% ABV; from pot still, 82% ABV

BARREL-ENTRY PROOF: Light rums (continuous columns), 65% ABV; heavy rums (batch kettle and pot stills), 55% ABV

MATURATION: American white oak previously used for bourbon and single malts. Diplomático ages its Single Vintage and Ambassador in Spanish sherry casks for additional time for what is called a "finish" after it's been in American oak. All Diplomático is aged for a minimum of 2 years in white oak, per country regulations. The brand's Reserva Exclusiva is aged for up to 12 years.

FILTRATION: All Diplomático rums are chill-filtered in filter plates, with these 2 exceptions: Diplomático Ambassador, which is filtered at room temperature, and Diplomático Blanco, which is charcoal filtered to remove its color and make it crystal clear.

COLOR ADDED: Yes

SUGAR ADDED: Venezuelan refined sugar is added to the barrel and aged the final months before bottling.

ABOVE AND OPPOSITE: *Diplomático stills.*
DIPLOMÁTICO RUM

DON PANCHO PORTFOLIO

LOCATION: Las Cabras, Pesé, in Herrera Province, Republic of Panama (many suggest that Don Pancho's older rums come from various distilleries)

WATER SOURCE: Natural local sources from about 10 months of rainfall

SOURCE MATERIAL: Proprietary molasses.

OFF-THE-STILL PROOF: 90% ABV

BARREL-ENTRY PROOF: 75% ABV

MATURATION: Heaven Hill, Buffalo Trace, or Jim Beam ex-bourbon American oak casks

FILTRATION: Cellulose plates

COLOR ADDED: 0.01–0.05 percent to standardize the batch

SUGAR ADDED: Yes

DON Q

LOCATION: San Juan, Puerto Rico

OFF-THE-STILL PROOF: 94.5% ABV

EL DORADO PORTFOLIO

LOCATION: East Bank, Demerara, Guyana, South America

DISTILLATION: Pot and column stills. Some products are blended, some are single pot.

SOURCE MATERIAL: Molasses, locally sourced along the coast

OFF-THE-STILL PROOF: 80% to 95% ABV

BARREL-ENTRY PROOF: 70% ABV

MATURATION: Used bourbon barrels except for special casks

COLOR ADDED: Small amount of caramel coloring to equalize color

SUGAR ADDED: Master distiller Shaun Caleb says there is no sugar additive, but says, "Any sugar detected is from the aging from fresh spirit or some of the spirit it's aged with. Only after blending." Multiple online reports have been published suggesting El Dorado rums contain sweeteners.

FLYING DUTCHMAN RUM

LOCATION: Baarle-Nassau, Netherlands

WATER SOURCE: Municipal water supply

SOURCE MATERIAL: Cane molasses with long slow fermentation (two weeks)

DISTILLATION: Double- or triple-distilled in pot stills before aging. 100% pot-still distillation.

OFF-THE-STILL PROOF: 74% to 76% ABV

BARREL-ENTRY PROOF: 60% ABV

MATURATION: Minimum one year for the Flying Dutchman #1, matured in 200-liter casks made from American oak (virgin and reused); minimum 3 years for the Flying Dutchman #3, with one-third of rum matured in 200-liter casks made from American oak (virgin and reused), one-third rum matured in 250-liter casks formerly used for Oloroso sherry, and one-third matured in 250-liter casks formerly used for Pedro Ximénez (PX) sherry; minimum 4 years for the Flying Dutchman Special 2012 PX, with 100% of rum matured in 250-liter casks formerly used for PX sherry.

FILTRATION: Normal sheet filtration

COLOR ADDED: None

SUGAR ADDED: None

FOURSQUARE PORTFOLIO

LOCATION: Four Roads, Barbados

WATER SOURCE: Coral stone well

DISTILLATION: Foursquare's distillation techniques vary per brand. They include single pot, blended, and column.

OFF-THE-STILL PROOF: Column, 94.5 to 94.8% ABV; pot, 82% ABV.

BARREL-ENTRY PROOF: 65% ABV

MATURATION: Ex-bourbon, port, Cognac, and sherry barrels

COLOR ADDED: Yes, for some releases

SUGAR ADDED: None

GOSLING'S

LOCATION: Bottled in Bermuda

WATER SOURCE: Bermuda rainwater

SOURCE MATERIAL: Molasses

DISTILLATION: A blend of pot and column distillates

OFF-THE-STILL PROOF: Approximately 79% ABV

BARREL-ENTRY PROOF: 60% and 62.5% ABV

MATURATION: Used bourbon barrels

FILTRATION: Carlson XE filter pads

COLOR ADDED: A small amount of caramel for consistency in appearance

SUGAR ADDED: None

HAMILTON

Ed Hamilton selects some of the world's best rums and places his name on the bottle. He only works with distillers who allow him to disclose the rum's origins, which many distillers and brokers forbid in fear of merchant bottlers trading on their names. Hamilton's bottlings include distilleries from Jamaica, Guyana, Martinique, and Saint Lucia. On his product fact sheets found at Caribbean-Spirits.com, Hamilton reveals much information about his brands. For example, on the St. Lucian Vendome Pot Still, he writes, "The collection bottled in Jan 2015 consists of 5, 7, 8, 9 and 10 year old rums aged in St Lucia and then shipped in the casks in which they were aged to Westfield, NY where they were bottled at cask strength (118–136 proof).... Two barrels of 7, 8 and 9 year old rum were selected to be bottled as single cask, cask strength rum and will be sold as complete barrels. The remaining barrels of each age were then batched and bottled under a batch number on the label indicated by the age followed by the month and year. 80115 is an 8 year old rum bottled in Jan 2015."

ISAUTIER RHUM

LOCATION: Réunion

WATER SOURCE: Reverse osmosis from Réunion

SOURCE MATERIAL: Réunion cane juice

OFF-THE-STILL PROOF: 89% ABV. The brand's agricoles are coming off the still at around 70% ABV. Between 2013 and 2016, variations between 69.2% ABV and 72.3% ABV.

BARREL-ENTRY PROOF: Same as off-the-still proof

FILTRATION: None

COLOR ADDED: None

SUGAR ADDED: None

J. BALLY

LOCATION: East Martinique

WATER SOURCE: Reverse osmosis from Martinique source

SOURCE MATERIAL: Fresh cane juice

OFF-THE-STILL PROOF: Degré de coulage AOC between 65 and 75, here about 72

BARREL-ENTRY PROOF: Unknown

MATURATION: Aged only in oak wood

FILTRATION: Neutral on cotton or cellulose < 0.1 μm for white rum and 2.5 μm for aged rum

COLOR ADDED: None

SUGAR ADDED: None

Mount Gay rum master blender Allen Smith blends pot-still and column-still rums to produce the widely distributed Mount Gay Rum. He is one of rum's most revered blenders.

MONTANYA

LOCATION: Crested Butte, Colorado

WATER SOURCE: Colorado Rocky Mountain spring and snowmelt-charged aquifer

SOURCE MATERIAL: Raw unrefined sugarcane. Regarding this rather unique material, founder Karen Hoskin says the onsite mill processes Louisiana cane one time. "That means pressing out the cane and separating 12 percent of that fresh juice into unrefined molasses and the other 88 percent into raw unrefined sugar cane. This has been crystallized and centrifuged one time, with no flocculant additives. Essentially, the water and bagasse have been removed. We also get the first press of the sugar cane, which is much like the extra-virgin olive oil is to the olive," Hoskin says. "Typical refined sugar cane goes through six more layers of processing than what we receive, and goes to the refinery after the mill. Ours does not."

DISTILLATION: Alembic copper pot stills.

OFF-THE-STILL PROOF: 85% ABV

BARREL-ENTRY PROOF: 85% ABV

MATURATION: 1 to 3 years

FILTRATION: Coconut-husk charcoal for only Platino, plate filtration for all three

COLOR ADDED: Trace amounts of caramelized Rocky Mountain honey

SUGAR ADDED: Honey. But Hoskin does not consider her honey an additive. "We don't think of our honey as an additive, but as a natural raw ingredient. Additives are typically . . . artificial flavorings, natural and artificial colorings, glycerin, propylene glycol, etc. but this may be a matter of semantics," she says.

MOUNT GAY

LOCATION: Saint Lucy, Barbados

WATER SOURCE: Onsite well

SOURCE MATERIAL: Sugarcane molasses

OFF-THE-STILL PROOF: Batch column is 97% ABV. Pot still is significantly lower, but the exact percentage is unknown. Mount Gay is a blend of aged pot and column distillates. Mount Gay does not disclose its percentages but says some 250 to 300 barrels go into a batch to bottle.

COLOR ADDED: Minimal

SUGAR ADDED: None, per country regulations

MUDDY RIVER DISTILLERY

LOCATION: Belmont, North Carolina

WATER SOURCE: Water filtration system

SOURCE MATERIAL: Molasses from sugarcane grown in Louisiana and Florida

DISTILLATION: Single run through a 5-plate reflux column still. Stills designed and built by founder.

OFF-THE-STILL PROOF: 90% ABV

BARREL-ENTRY PROOF: 90% ABV

MATURATION: One year in a virgin barrel for Queen Charlotte's Reserve rum. Two-plus months for Silver, Coconut, and Spiced.

FILTRATION: Mild carbon and sediment filtration

COLOR ADDED: None

SUGAR ADDED: Minimal cane sugar added to Coconut and Spiced Carolina Rums only.

NEISSON DISTILLERY

LOCATION: Le Carbet, Martinique

SOURCE MATERIAL: Fresh sugarcane juice

OFF-THE-STILL PROOF: 72% ABV

MATURATION: Several types of barrels, including French oak and used bourbon barrels. For the Neisson Reserve Special, the rhum ages for 3 to 6 years in used bourbon barrels and is finished in used Cognac barrels.

NOVO FOGO CACHAÇA

LOCATION: Morretes, Brazil

WATER SOURCE: Underground water

SOURCE MATERIAL: Estate-grown sugarcane juice

DISTILLATION: Single-pot alembic distillation.

OFF-THE-STILL PROOF: 48% ABV to 54% ABV

BARREL-ENTRY PROOF: Enters the barrel from the still

MATURATION: Used American oak barrels

FILTRATION: No chill filtration

COLOR ADDED: None

SUGAR ADDED: None

OKSEN

LOCATION: Le Canon, Aquitaine, France

Oksen is a line of ultrapremium flavored rums that uses fresh-fruit infusions to reach its flavor profiles. Launched in 2009, the owner's plan was to play with the aromatic range of spices, berries, and fruits through exclusively natural, slow, and rigorous macerations in agricultural rhum from Martinique, but sublimating all the scents of only one ingredient at a time. The first one is made with entire cinnamon sticks. The second was the use of "split vanilla," which ripens on its liana until the pod opens. The third infusion uses banana from Ecuador. The fourth is the first blending infusion of whole orange, which is slower to macerate, and mocha coffee.

Coffee beans are a common flavoring agent in flavored rum.

OPTHIMUS AND SOUTH BAY

LOCATION: No single distillery. The producer purchases from distilleries in Panama, Guatemala, Nicaragua, Dominican Republic, Trinidad and Tobago, and the French and English Caribbean islands. They're additionally aged and blended in Hato Nuevo, Dominican Republic.

WATER SOURCE: Purified Dominican water is used for dilution.

SOURCE MATERIAL: Molasses

OFF-THE-STILL PROOF: 95% ABV from Panama, Guatemala, Nicaragua, and Dominican Republic distilleries; 75% ABV from Trinidad and Tobago and other distilleries in the French and English Caribbean islands.

BARREL-ENTRY PROOF: Varies by expression

MATURATION: According to the company, 15, 18, 21, or 25 years in American oak barrels previously used for bourbon. The 25-Year-Old Port Finish is rested for an additional several months in empty ex-port barrels from the Graham's winery in Jerez. The 25-Year-Old Malt Finish is rested for an additional several months in empty ex-single-malt-whiskey barrels from the Tomatin Distillery in Scotland.

COLOR ADDED: Caramel is added to obtain uniformity of color between the different production batches.

SUGAR ADDED: Pedro Ximénez wine at 17% ABV, caramel, vanilla, muscat, and water

PARCE RUM

LOCATION: Colombia

WATER SOURCE: Deionized Colombian water

SOURCE MATERIAL: Both sugarcane-juice and molasses based

OFF-THE-STILL PROOF: Between 80% and 93% ABV

BARREL-ENTRY PROOF: Between 70% and 75% ABV

MATURATION: 100% used bourbon barrels

FILTRATION: Polish filtration as needed

COLOR ADDED: Yes

SUGAR ADDED: Cane syrup

PHRAYA

LOCATION: Sangsom Distillery and Nakhon Pathom Distillery, Thailand

WATER SOURCE: Tha Chin River, Nakhon Pathom, Thailand

SOURCE MATERIAL: Molasses derived from locally grown sugarcane

DISTILLATION: Column stills with output of 9,000 to 40,000 liters per day

OFF-THE-STILL PROOF: 95% ABV

BARREL-ENTRY PROOF: 65% ABV

MATURATION: Ex-bourbon and ex-rum barrels

FILTRATION: Paper filter

COLOR ADDED: Caramel color added as needed for consistency

SUGAR ADDED: Unknown

PRICHARD'S

LOCATION: Whites Creek, Tennessee

WATER SOURCE: Teal Hollow spring water

SOURCE MATERIAL: Grade A premium table-grade molasses, 90 percent to 95 percent, fermentable sugars from Louisiana

DISTILLATION: Pot or column still. Vendome copper pot still. 550-gallon main line stripper and a 110-gallon spirit still.

OFF-THE-STILL PROOF: 72.5% ABV

BARREL-ENTRY PROOF: 72.5% ABV

MATURATION: White oak barrels from Arkansas with a 3-millimeter Alligator Char, usually of 15 gallons. Minimum 5 years to as much as 15 years.

FILTRATION: Not chilled

COLOR ADDED: None

SUGAR ADDED: None

PRIVATEER

LOCATION: Ipswich, Massachusetts

SOURCE MATERIAL: Three types—molasses from Florida and Louisiana, boil cane, and cane crystals, fermented for six days using both natural and inoculated yeast

DISTILLATION: Pot and column

OFF-THE-STILL PROOF: 85% to 94% ABV

BARREL-ENTRY PROOF: 55% ABV

MATURATION: Used and new American charred oak, as well as used rum and Cognac barrels

COLOR ADDED: None

SUGAR ADDED: None

PUERTO ANGEL

LOCATION: Oaxaca, Mexico

WATER SOURCE: Mountain water

SOURCE MATERIAL: Organically grown sugarcane and the resulting fresh cane juice. Cane is pressed within 24 hours after cutting. Rum is certified organic.

DISTILLATION: Pot or column still; copper pot stills

OFF-THE-STILL PROOF: 50% ABV

BARREL-ENTRY PROOF: 50% ABV

MATURATION: Missouri oak barrels

FILTRATION: Charcoal

COLOR ADDED: None

SUGAR ADDED: None

PUSSER'S PRODUCTION

LOCATION: Headquartered in Charleston, South Carolina, but its rum is from all over the world.

WATER SOURCE: Deionized

SOURCE MATERIAL: Molasses

DISTILLATION: The product of five stills, three in Guyana and two in Trinidad

BARREL-ENTRY PROOF: 66% to 68.8% ABV

FILTRATION: Charcoal

COLOR ADDED: Liquid caramel 525 Class 1 (less than 0.2%)

SUGAR ADDED: Various reports indicate Pusser's contains additives.

RANK WILDCAT SPIRITS PORTFOLIO

LOCATION: Lafayette, Louisiana, United States

WATER SOURCE: Chicot Aquifer, a massive and ancient subterranean lake beneath Acadiana

SOURCE MATERIAL: Mixture of raw sugar, cane syrup, and molasses

DISTILLATION: Handmade still kettle outfitted with a custom column

OFF-THE-STILL PROOF: 91% ABV

BARREL-ENTRY PROOF: 55% ABV

MATURATION: Sweet Crude is a white rum and is proofed and bottled right from the still. Black Gold is aged with hand-charred American white oak staves harvested from whiskey barrels. After close monitoring, when the staves have done their job, the rum finishes its maturation in 10-gallon charred oak barrels.

FILTRATION: None

COLOR ADDED: None

SUGAR ADDED: None

Sweet Crude rum.

RHUM BARBANCOURT

LOCATION: Port-au-Prince, Haiti

WATER SOURCE: Well

SOURCE MATERIAL: Sugarcane juice

OFF-THE-STILL PROOF: 85% ABV

BARREL ENTRY PROOF: 62.5% ABV

MATURATION: French oak

FILTRATION: Yes, before bottling

COLOR ADDED: Natural caramel

SUGAR ADDED: None

RICHLAND RUM

LOCATION: Richland, Georgia, United States

WATER SOURCE: Underground aquifer, tapped by well

SOURCE MATERIAL: Syrup from estate-grown cane

DISTILLATION: Pot still.

OFF-THE-STILL PROOF: 80% to 85% ABV

BARREL-ENTRY PROOF: 60% ABV

MATURATION: New, charred, American oak barrels

FILTRATION: None

COLOR ADDED: None

RON ABUELO PORTFOLIO

LOCATION: Hacienda San Isidro, Pesé, Panama

WATER SOURCE: Groundwater reserves

SOURCE MATERIAL: Local molasses

DISTILLATION: Column still

OFF-THE-STILL PROOF: 75% to 85% ABV

BARREL-ENTRY PROOF: 60% to 68% ABV

MATURATION: Bourbon barrels that have held bourbon for 3 to 5 years. Añejo is matured for 3 to 4 years; the 7-Year-Old is matured for up to 7 years. The 12-Year-Old is matured for up to 11 years, and Centuria is matured for up to 30 years; in their last year of maturation, both rums are transferred to a "new" bourbon barrel at 48 % ABV (96 proof).

COLOR ADDED: Caramel

SUGAR ADDED: Yes

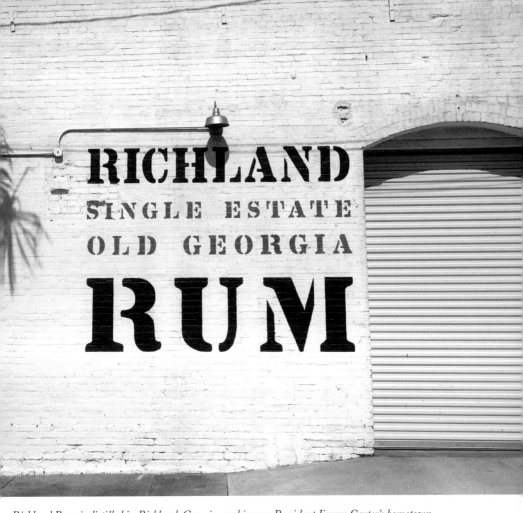

Richland Rum is distilled in Richland, Georgia, and is near President Jimmy Carter's hometown.

RON MONTERO PORTFOLIO

LOCATION: Motril, Granada, Spain

WATER SOURCE: Sierra Nevada

SOURCE MATERIAL: Molasses

DISTILLATION: Unknown

OFF-THE-STILL PROOF: 80% and 90% ABV

BARREL-ENTRY PROOF: 60% ABV

MATURATION: Virgin American oak barrels

FILTRATION: Charcoal

COLOR ADDED: A few drops to homogenize color

SUGAR ADDED: None

PLANTATION PORTFOLIO

LOCATION: Rum is purchased throughout the Caribbean and additionally aged and bottled in France.

Plantation is a merchant-bottler brand owned by Maison Ferrand, the parent company of Citadelle Gin and Pierre Ferrand Cognac. The company purchases barrels from major rum regions and has them shipped in barrel or tanker to France, where master blender Alexandre Gabriel blends them using the technique he calls "dosage" and "élevage." Thus, the technical specs for these rums are more difficult to trace. Some releases, such as the Barbados edition, will include rum from more than one distillery, so these products are really about the blending and not necessarily the distillation.

Alexandre Gabriel founded Pierre Ferrand and added Plantation rum to his portfolio in 2006. His rum has become one of the most respected merchant-bottled products in all of spirits. Gabriel purchases bulk rum from various distillers and bottles them. He is likely the most respected proponent of additives in rum.

ST. GEORGE SPIRITS

LOCATION: Alameda, California, United States

WATER SOURCE: Hetch Hetchy Reservoir (Sierra Nevada Mountains)

SOURCE MATERIAL: California-grown sugarcane

OFF-THE-STILL PROOF: 65% to 69% ABV

BARREL-ENTRY PROOF: 55% ABV

MATURATION: For St. George California Agricole Rum—stainless steel, 6 months; for St. George California Reserve Agricole Rum—French oak, 3 to 4 years

FILTRATION: Paper pads in a plate-and-frame housing

COLOR ADDED: None

SUGAR ADDED: None

SAINT JAMES

LOCATION: Sainte Marie, Martinique

WATER SOURCE: Reverse-osmosis water

SOURCE MATERIAL: Fresh cane juice

OFF-THE-STILL PROOF: 72% ABV

BARREL-ENTRY PROOF: Unknown

MATURATION: Aging only in oak wood

FILTRATION: Neutral on cotton or cellulose < 0.1 μm for white rum and 2.5 μm for aging rum

COLOR ADDED: None

SUGAR ADDED: None

ST. NICHOLAS ABBEY

LOCATION: Saint Peter Parish, Barbados

WATER SOURCE: Reverse osmosis

SOURCE MATERIAL: Cane syrup

DISTILLATION: Pot-and-column hybrid

OFF-THE-STILL PROOF: 92% ABV

BARREL-ENTRY PROOF: 65% ABV

COLOR ADDED: Natural coloring

SUGAR ADDED: None

WORTHY PARK ESTATE

LOCATION: Worthy Park Estate, Saint Catherine, Jamaica

WATER SOURCE: Well water through limestone aquifer

SOURCE MATERIAL: Molasses produced from the sugar factory at the estate

DISTILLATION: Pot

OFF-THE-STILL PROOF: 84% to 85% ABV

BARREL-ENTRY PROOF: 65% to 70% ABV

MATURATION: Once-used American white oak barrels, tropical-aged at the Worthy Park Estate

FILTRATION: Charcoal

COLOR ADDED: None

SUGAR ADDED: None

ZACAPA PORTFOLIO

LOCATION: Distilleries in Tulula and San Andrés Villa Seca Retalhuleu, Guatemala

WATER SOURCE: In every plant, water comes from natural private wells.

SOURCE MATERIAL: First-crushed virgin sugarcane

DISTILLATION: Column

OFF-THE-STILL PROOF: 88% to 92% ABV

BARREL-ENTRY PROOF: 60% ABV

MATURATION: RZC 23 American White Oak, once recharred American white oak, sherry, and Pedro Ximénez, solera-system aging.

FILTRATION: En frío (cold filtration)

COLOR ADDED: Caramel, only when required to standardize color

SUGAR ADDED: Yes

APPENDIX B

Rum Resources

There are many rum resources availalable online and in your local bookstore. These websites, periodicals, and books will help you further your rum love.

WEBSITES

RumRatings   www.rumratings.com
Features consumer ratings. Some reviews are very cogent, while others appear to be brand friendly. Either way, the site serves as rum's Yelp, an unfiltered voice for rum reviewers.

Cocktail Wonk   www.cocktailwonk.com
Matt Pietrek, AKA Cocktail Wonk, is America's foremost rum blogger. His work serves the geek's interests and he pulls no punches in his criticism.

Ministry of Rum   www.ministryofrum.com
Started by rum writer turned brand owner Ed Hamilton, the Ministry of Rum presents highly technical information on all rums, tasting notes, and a searchable database for all rums.

Rum Project   www.rumproject.com
This is where you go to read the rum rumors and talk dirt on brands you don't like.

Rob's Rum Guide   www.robsrum.com
A friendly voice and fun read about brands and news.

PERIODICALS

Got Rum?	www.gotrum.com
Imbibe	www. imbibemagazine.com
Cigar Aficianado	www. cigaraficionado.com
Distiller	www. distiller.com
Cigar & Spirits	www. cigarandspirits.com
Wine Enthusiast	www. winemag.com

BIBLIOGRAPHY

INTERVIEWS

Richard Seale

Alexandre Gabriel

Ed Hamilton

Kenneth McCoy

Kate Price

Max Solano

Bailey Pryor

Simon Warren

Andrew Hassell

Shaun Caleb

Jim Driscoll

Joy Spence

BOOKS AND PUBLICATIONS

Ashley, John. *Memoirs and Considerations Concerning the Trade and Revenues of the British Colonies in America. With Proposals for Rendering those Colonies more Beneficial to Great Britain.* London: C. Corbett, 1751.

Cate, Martin. *Smuggler's Cove: Exotic Cocktails, Rum and the Cult of Tiki.* New York: Ten Speed Press, 2016.

Curtis, Wayne. *And a Bottle of Rum: A History of the New World in Ten Cocktails.* New York: Broadway Books, 2007.

Daniels, Christian, Joseph Needham, and Nicholas K. Menzies, *Science and Civilisation in China.* Cambridge: Cambridge Press, 1996.

Dossie, Robert. *An Essay on Spirituous Liquors; with Regard to their Effects on Health*. London: Printed for J. Ridley, 1770.

Eight Practical Treatises on the Cultivation of the Sugar Cane. Jamaica: Jordan & Osborn, 1843.

Hansen, Valerie, and Ken Curtis. *Voyages in World History*, vol. 2. Boston: Cengage Learning, 2015.

A Letter to a Member of Parliament on the Importance of the American Colonies [electronic resource]: and the Best Means of making them most Useful to the Mother Country. London: Printed for J. Scott, 1757.

Williams, Ian. *Rum: A Social and Sociable History of the Real Spirit of 1776*. New York: Nation Books, 2005.

Wondrich, David. *Punch: The Delights (and Dangers) of the Flowing Bowl*. New York: Perigree, 2010.

SEMINARS

Burrell, Ian, Alexandre Gabriel, Ben Jones, Richard Seale, and Roberto Serrales. "When Is Rum not a Rum?" Tales of the Cocktail, New Orleans: July 20, 2016.

ACKNOWLEDGMENTS

I'LL NEVER FORGET THE WALK MY FAMILY AND I WERE ON when I was offered a two-book agreement from Quarto. I questioned whether I could write two books at once. (The other was *Bourbon: The Rise, Fall, and Rebirth of an American Whiskey*.) My wife, Jaclyn, looked me square in the eye and said: "Are you a writer?" "Yes," I said. "Then, you can write both," she concluded.

And so, without her faith in me, this book never gets written. Of course, she loves rum, so she may have had other motives.

Thank you to Richard Seale, Jim Romdall, and Matt Pietrek for reading *Rum Curious* in manuscript either in full or in parts. Martin Cate, I appreciate your beautiful foreword and faith in my rum work more than I can express. Your rummy blessings meant the world to me.

Thank you to Louisville bar owner Matthew Landan for opening up his private Cuban rum collection for me to sample.

To Erik Gilg, thank you for continuing to give me book opportunities.

My agent, Linda Konner, helped make this happen.

A big thanks to my local rum watering hole, Citizen 7, and Adam Sabin for allowing me to use their bar for my photoshoot. Adam's mad skills with the shaker were fun to shoot. I am grateful to Mike Godfrey for his hand modeling during the cigar shoot.

I also could not have written this book without my friend Mark Leppart obtaining the rum and organizing my tasting room. It's not easy tasting more than four hundred rums, some of which didn't make this book, and Mark helped me organize it all! And of course, to Cuba and the United States, if you guys didn't get your shit worked out, publishers wouldn't be interested in rum. So, thanks.

INDEX

OPPOSITE: *The all-important aging process.* GETTY IMAGES

232 • INDEX

Image Credits

ADRIAN KEOGH: 30

ALAMY STOCK PHOTO: 7 (Archivart), 160–161
    (Emma Lee), 238 (PhotoCuisine RM)

APPLETON ESTATE JAMAICA RUM: 21

BAYOU RUM: 202

BRIDGEMAN IMAGES: 2–3 (Private Collection/
    Peter Newark Pictures); 4 (Manchester
    Art Gallery, UK); 10 (Photo © PVDE),
    14–15 (Bibliothèque Nationale, Paris,
    France); 24–25 (Yale Center for British
    Art, Paul Mellon Fund); 26 (© Look and
    Learn); 201 (Private Collection/Archives
    Charmet); 204 (The Stapleton Collec-
    tion); 236, top left, top right (DaTo
    Images), bottom left (Pictures from
    History), and bottom right (Photo ©
    GraphicaArtis); 237; 240

DIPLOMÁTICO RUM 206, 207

GETTY IMAGES: 184 (GUIZIOU FRANCK),
    198 (Victor Kayfetz/Three Lions), 199
    (Photo by Roper/Topical Press Agency),
    230 (Marvin del Cid)

HOUSE OF AGRICOLE: 81, 118

LIBRARY OF CONGRESS: 29, 32, 36, 45, 47, 51,
    77, 82–83

PAUL WAGTOUICZ: 180

THE REAL MCCOY SPIRITS CO.: 52

SCOTT SCORSOLINI: 239

SHUTTERSTOCK: 12–13 (Jakob Fischer), 31
    (Everett Historical), 112 (Brent
    Hofacker), 164–165 (marchello74), 172
    (merc67), 196–197 (Kkulikov)

UNITED STATES DEPARTMENT OF
    AGRICULTURE, AGRICULTURAL
    RESEARCH SERVICE: 43

FOLLOWING SPREAD: *Vintage advertisements for rum and for one of its sources, Jamaica.*
BRIDGEMAN IMAGES

RUM LA NEGRITA

MONOPOLE

P. Bardinet

LIMOGES

MÉDAILLE D'OR.
Expⁿ Univᵉˡˡᵉ de Paris 1889

RHUM CHAUVET

PROPRIÉTÉ
DE LA Cⁱᵉ DES ANTILLES

RON
MULATA
de CUBA

EJO BLANCO

JAMAICA

THE GEM
of the
TROPICS

BEAUTIFUL HEALTHY ACCESSIBLE
TICKETS BY ALL
STEAMSHIP LINES HERE

Next time you
make an Old-Fashioned,
rum instead of whiskey.
You're in for a
great surprise!

86 PROOF
GENERAL DISTILLERIES CORP., BOSTON, MASS.

ABOUT THE AUTHOR

MULTIBOOK BEST-SELLING AUTHOR FRED MINNICK judges rum at the San Francisco World Spirits Competition and covers it for several international publications. He is a two-time Tales of the Cocktail Spirited Award finalist and frequently appears in the media, including NPR, the *New York Times*, CBS *This Morning*, *Esquire*, and many others. View his work at www.FredMinnick.com.

OPPOSITE: *Bottles being filled at the Havana Club Museum of Rum.* ALAMY STOCK PHOTO
FOLLOWING PAGE: *A French label for punch with rum, circa 1900.* BRIDGEMAN IMAGES

A New Map of the ENGLISH PLANTATIONS in
AMERICA
both Continent and Ilands,
Shewing their true Situation and distance, from
England or one with another.
By Robert Morden, at the Atlas, in Cornhill
near the Royal Exchange, and William Berry
at the Globe, between York House and the New
Exchange in the Strand, LONDON.

FELIS LAKE

MARY

VIRGINIA

Dogs Indians

The Richbockans

F L O R I = D A

C A R O = L I = N A

THE GOLFE OF
MEXICO

GOLPE OF FLORIDA

la Florida

Bahama

New Providence

JAMAICA

MAR DEL

ZUR

Costarica

NICARAGVA

H O N D V R A S

Golfo d. Honduras

Guaxaca

PA:

Chiapa

Thascala

CO

N